DEFENDING THE FAITH:
TRIALS AND GREAT DEBATES IN JEWISH HISTORY

DEFENDING THE FAITH:

TRIALS AND GREAT DEBATES IN JEWISH HISTORY

By
Rabbi Ron Isaacs

Ktav Publishing House, Inc.

Distributed by
Ktav Publishing House, Inc.
900 Jefferson Street
Hoboken, NJ 07030
201-963-9524 FAX 201-963-0102
Email orders@ktav.com
Web www.ktav.com

ISBN 0-88125-714-1

Contents

Introduction

Disputations between Jews and non-Jews were frequent in ancient and medieval times. Religious differences have at all times induced serious-minded people to exchange their views in order to win opponents over to their own side by appeals to reason. In the Midrash, Abraham is represented as having a religious debate with Nimrod. The talmudic-midrashic literature contains many examples of disputations between Jews and adherents of other religions. In a later period, the friendliness and good humor of these religious discussions gave way to remorseless fanaticism directed not only against Jews and Judaism but also against their sacred literature.

In Alexandria, Egypt, disputations and arguments between Jews and pagans were quite frequent.

The first actual disputation before a worldly ruler took place at Alexandria in 150 B.C.E. between Andronicus ben Meshullam, a Judean, and Sabbaeus and Dositheos, Samaritans. The argument concerned a Bible text that the Samaritans claimed had been omitted by the Jews in the Greek translation of the Bible.

In the middle of the thirteenth century, twenty-four cart-loads of the Talmud were burned in the public square of Paris. A generation later, a converted Jew by the name of Pablo Christiani induced the king of Aragon to compel Rabbi Moses Nachmanides to join him in a public disputation. Nachmanides' disputation with Pablo, which took place at Barcelona in 1263, lasted four days. The debate concerned the concept of the Messiah and took place in the presence of the king and many dignitaries. The issues included whether the Hebrew prophets had prophesied a Messiah of divine or human birth, and whether the Messiah had already appeared.   Nachmanides declared that he could not believe that the Messiah had come so long as the promised cessation of warfare had not been fulfilled. Although he had been promised immunity and the right of free expression in the course of the debate, Nachmanides was soon summoned before the king's court and tried for blasphemy. He was condemned to two years in exile, and his account of the contest, which he had written for the bishop of Gerona, was burned.

In the early part of the fifteenth century, a disputation in Tortosa, northern Spain, lasted more than eighteen months. After sixty-nine sessions, the verdict was announced: the Talmud was condemned and a variety of hostile laws against the Jews were enacted. During this time the pope exerted constant physical and moral pressure upon the Jews to become apostates.

Defending the Faith: Trials and Great Debates in Jewish History presents some of the famous biblical and religious disputes throughout the centuries, and allows students an opportunity to role-play and debate the issues in a classroom setting. This volume features fourteen debates and trials from Jewish history (some from the actual records, others inferred from what is known about certain historical events). The debates include the case of Brother Daniel, the disputation of Tortosa, the excommunication of Spinoza, the Dreyfus Trial and publication of "J'accuse" by Émile Zola, and the U.S. Supreme Court rulings on the Neo-Nazi rally in Skokie, Illinois. The book affords students with an opportunity to hold simulated trials of several problematic events in the Bible in which a character's behavior is under scrutiny for disloyalty. These stories include Jeremiah's "treasonous" sermon on the Temple Mount, the ten spies who demoralize a people, the sacrifice of Isaac, the fall of Adam and Eve, the sin of the golden calf, and the story of Joseph and his jealous brothers. Finally, the volume presents an opportunity to debate the Hillel and Shammai talmudic argument vis-à-vis how to light a hanukkiah, a simulated debate between the Hellenists and the pietists of Maccabean times, and a debate regarding a desire among some to change the age of bar/bat mitzvah from thirteen to sixteen.

It is my hope that this book will help students to improve their understanding of these significant events in Jewish history, while at the same time giving them an opportunity to experience history in a novel way through the process of trial and debating. The purpose of the debates is to allow students to use their newly gained knowledge about a particular case story and to "live" it, deeply and imaginatively. In essence, the debate is designed to help participants feel the event, better identify with the personalities, and sense their dilemmas, hopes, and expectations.

I once again want to thank our students in Temple Sholom Hebrew High School for allowing us to field-test this course, and the school's beloved teacher David Kritz, who gave this course his commitment and inspiration.

Rabbi Ron Isaacs

1

The Case of Brother Daniel

1940s
Israel

BACKGROUND

The case that you are about to study will deal with one of the most important questions in all of Judaism: Who is a Jew? According to the dictionary, a Jew is "a person whose religion is Judaism." The question of Jewish identity first arose after the nineteenth-century emancipation of the Jews of western and central Europe and the spread of the Haskalah, that is, the Jewish Enlightenment. As some Jews became alienated from Judaism and attempted to join the gentile majority culturally and in some cases religiously, Jewish identity became a problem. Prior to that time, of course, Jewish self-identification had not been an issue. In biblical times, the Hebrew people derived their identity from the tradition that they were descendants of Abraham, Isaac, and Jacob, and heirs to a religion which went back to the revelation at Mount Sinai. To live in Israel was an integral part of their identity, and as long as one lived in the Land, one was a member of the Hebrew people. Only by moving abroad did people lose their share in "the inheritance of God" (1 Samuel 26:19), that is, their identification with the Hebrew religion and people.

1

The foreigner who came to settle in the biblical land of Israel was absorbed into the Hebrew community. Internally, distinctions were made by tribal affiliation, especially between the kohanim (priestly descendants of Aaron), the Levites who served the kohanim, and the common people, the Israelites. Descent was reckoned through the patrilineal line, which meant that every person belonged to the tribe of his or her father. The mother's ethnic origin was disregarded. When a Hebrew man married a non-Hebrew woman, as did the sons of Jacob, Moses, and others, his children were considered Hebrews!

The biblical Hebrews designated themselves *ivrim*, "Hebrews," in relation to other peoples. Abraham is called a Hebrew in Genesis 14:13, and the prophet Jonah, when asked by his gentile shipmates to identify himself, answers, *ani ivri*—"I am a Hebrew, and I fear the God of heaven" (Jonah 1:9).

Once the descendants of the Hebrews began to live in the Diaspora (i.e., outside of Israel), they were known as *yehudim*, or "Jews" (Esther 2:5). Throughout this period, the identity of the Hebrews, whether called *ivrim*, *yehudim*, *b'nai Yisrael*, or *Yisrael*, or by one of the tribal designations, was never in doubt. The Hebrew religion, Hebrew peoplehood, and the Hebrew language were the threefold identity—and the threefold barrier—separating Hebrews from gentiles.

With the Babylonian exile (586 B.C.E.), the situation began to change. Geographical unity was lost. In the countries of the Diaspora, the Jews generally adopted the languages of their non-Jewish environment, but their identity remained clear-cut due to the power of the Jewish religion and the Jewish historical and cultural tradition. As late as the nineteenth century, Eastern European Jews, who constituted the overwhelming majority of the Jewish people, differed from the non-Jews of their countries in religion, traditions, behavior, language, dress, values, and world outlook. The question of whether one was or was not a Jew simply could not arise.

In relation to this reality the Jewish legal definition of a Jew as a person either born to a Jewish mother or formally converted had little practical significance. The first part of this rule was invoked in cases in which a Jewish woman was raped by a gentile (as happened during the pogroms). Any child born of such a union was considered a Jew. As for conversion, the low status and frequent victimization of the Jews until their emancipation made conversion to Judaism most unattractive.

This situation also meant that it was almost impossible for a Jew to leave Judaism. True, both Christianity and Islam welcomed Jewish converts, and put considerable pressure on Jews to adopt their faiths. But for Jews to leave their ancestral religion meant breaking with family and a whole social environment. And even in rare cases when a Jew denied Judaism, in the eyes of Jewish law he was not a Christian or a Muslim but a sinful Jew.

The solid framework of Jewish identity began to crack once the Haskalah spread among the Jews. For many "enlighteners" the culture of the non-Jews, particularly in Germany, France, and England, appeared more attractive than traditional Judaism. The more enchanted they became with the non-Jewish culture, the more indifferent they became toward Judaism. Many converted to Christianity, while others simply turned their backs on their Jewish heritage.

It was in connection with and among the Jewish apostates that the question of who is a Jew arose. They, the Jewish "doubters," were plagued by the ambiguity of their position. Was the Jew who had nothing to do with religion and community, or even had converted, still a Jew? Did the attitude of the convert toward Judaism affect his identity? This last question is relevant because quite a number of converts became notorious Jew haters (Karl Marx is a famous case in point).

Assimilation, with the problems it creates for both individual Jews and the Jewish community, is a Diaspora phenomenon. Here, Jews live as a minority in the midst of a non-Jewish majority possessed of an attractive culture. In Israel, where Jews are the majority, Jewish alienation from Judaism does not exist. This does not mean, however, that Israel is not plagued by the question of who is a Jew. Jewishness in Israel is quite a problem due to several factors. One is that among most Israeli Jews the traditional Jewish religious consciousness has been replaced by a new Israeli self-awareness in which not religion but nationhood—country, language, and culture—plays the central role.

Another factor is the rigorous position of the Israeli rabbinate. In Israel, the Orthodox rabbinate, with the help of its close allies, the religious parties, has been able to gain control of all official religious functions and has the power to decide the question of who is a Jew. Israel's Law of Return, one of the first laws enacted by the state, provides that every Jew has the right to settle in Israel and automatically become a citizen. In this connection the status of converts to Judaism and of communities such as Ethiopian Jewry became a stumbling block. The Israeli rabbinate does not recognize the validity of conversions carried out by Conservative, Reform, and Reconstructionist rabbis, and has attempted to bar such converts from invoking the Law of Return. This problem has created a great deal of tension between the Israeli Orthodox and the American Conservative, Reform, and Reconstructionist rabbinates. In 1984, Israel's rabbinate required that Ethiopian Jews, if they wanted to marry, had to undergo a symbolic conversion ritual. Public outcry followed, since for centuries the Ethiopian Jews had preserved their own form of the Jewish religion.

The foregoing should make it clear that Jewish identity has two separate but interlocking aspects. To be a Jew one must define oneself as a Jew, but also be so defined by others. The "others" can include individuals in one's immediate social environment, the community at large, official communal institutions (such as the rabbinate), or even non-Jewish society. It seems that only if the self-definition coincides with the definition by these others can one be considered a "real" Jew.

In 1958, the "Who is a Jew" issue came to light in the famous Brother Daniel case. Brother Daniel, a Carmelite monk living in a monastery in Haifa, petitioned Israel's High Court of Justice to become a citizen of Israel as provided for by the Law of Return. Brother Daniel had been born in Poland in 1922 to Jewish parents named Rufeisen, and at his circumcision was given the first name Oswald. He was reared and educated as a Jew in every respect, and was active in a Zionist youth movement in preparation for immigrating to Israel. During World War II he escaped a Nazi prison and evaded recapture by using forged documents certifying that he was a German Christian. Exploiting his Christian identity, he joined the anti-Nazi underground and saved many Jews by warning them of German extermination plans. In fleeing the Nazis he entered a Christian convent in 1942 and there converted to Christianity. Following the war he became a monk and entered the Carmelite order, knowing they had a monastery in Palestine. He never relinquished his aspiration to live in the Land of Israel.

Brother Daniel applied for Israeli citizenship in 1958 under the Law of Return, arguing that according to Jewish law a person born a Jew always remains a Jew. His lawyer recited the talmudic dictum: "A Jew, even if he has sinned, remains a Jew" (Sanhedrin 44a) and contended that even the most Orthodox Jew could not deny that Brother Daniel was a Jew.

DECISION
The High Court of Justice ruled that the term "Jew" in the Law of Return has a secular meaning. As it is understood by the ordinary person, a Jew who has become Christian is not a Jew. Thus in refusing to accept the halakhic (i.e., Jewish legal) definition of Jew, the High Court gave "Jew" a nationalist definition, reflecting this healthy instinct of the Jewish people and its thirst for survival.

DEBATE
You the students will now have a chance to simulate the case of Brother Daniel. A simulation is a dramatization of an event in which there is an attempt to portray some selected elements that have not actually occurred. The power of simulation was brought compellingly to anyone who watched the telecasts of the astronauts' voyages into space. The viewer was impressed by the fact that every conceivable eventuality was rehearsed beforehand. Simulation is able to bring future events before us so that we can prepare for them. Just as simulation brought future events into the immediacy of present experience, the dispute simulations are designed to help you bring past events into the living reality of the pre-

sent. The purpose of debating the case of Brother Daniel is to allow you, the participants, to have an opportunity to use your newly gained knowledge about the case to live it deeply, imaginatively, and intensely. The debate is designed to help you feel the event, identify with the personalities, sense their dilemmas and choices, their hopes and expectations.

In this simulated debate the participants are Brother Daniel and the members of the High Court. You also will want to choose a defense attorney for Brother Daniel, who will help to argue his case. You may likely also want to have some friends of Brother Daniel to testify on his behalf.

Following is some review information, called Fast Facts, as well as some additional information that will help the participants prepare for the debate.

Fast Facts

1. Jewishness in Israel is a problem due to a number of factors. One is that among many Israeli Jews the traditional Jewish religious consciousness has been replaced by a new Israeli self-awareness in which not religion but nationhood—country, language, and culture—plays the central role.

2. Israel has an Orthodox chief rabbi. Because he is Orthodox, the status of converts to Judaism and of traditional but exotic Jewish communities, such as that of the Ethiopian Jews, becomes a stumbling block. The rabbinate does not currently recognize the validity of conversions carried out by Reform, Conservative, and Reconstructionist rabbis, and has attempted to bar such converts from invoking the Law of Return.

3. Many Jews of questionable status have been made to undergo a symbolic conversion.

4. Jewish identity has two separate but interlocking aspects. To be a Jew one must define oneself as a Jew but also be so defined by others. The others can include individuals in one's immediate social environment, the community at large, official communal institutions (such as the rabbinate), or even gentile society. It works best if the self-definition coincides with the definition by these others so that one may be considered a Jew beyond a shadow of a doubt.

5. In 1939, the British Parliament issued a White Paper limiting Jewish immigration to Palestine to only 75,000 people over a five-year period. So, from 1939 to 1944, only 15,000 Jews per year were permitted to enter Palestine legally. This law came at a time when over six million Jews were being murdered in Europe by the Nazis. In 1950, Israel enacted the Law of Return, which states that upon arriving on Israeli soil a Jew is entitled to the rights of full citizenship if he or she so chooses. On the other hand, for a non-Jew citizenship is not automatic but requires a process of naturalization similar to that in the United States. Related to the Law of Return is the Law of Population Registration, enacted in 1949, which requires every inhabitant of Israel over sixteen years old to carry identification declaring nationality, religion, and citizenship.

6. The Reform movement's rabbinate in the 1980s passed the patrilineal-descent vote, which states that not only is a child born of a Jewish mother Jewish but a child born only of a Jewish father (but raised as a Jew) is also a Jew.

7. Another landmark decision of Israel's High Court led to the first legislative amendment to the Law of Return. A lieutenant commander in the Israeli navy, Benjamin Shalit,

born in Israel, married a non-Jewish woman in Scotland. After the marriage they settled in Israel, where Shalit's wife became a naturalized citizen. She never converted to Judaism, but the Shalits reared their two children like other Israeli children, instilling in them loyalty to the Jewish people. When Commander Shalit filled out the questionnaire for the Population Registry for his first-born child, in the space for nationality he entered the word "Jewish" and left the space for religion blank. The registrar of the Ministry of Interior struck out the entry for nationality and in the space for religion wrote "Father Jewish; mother non-Jewish." When the second child was born, Commander Shalit did not fill in the spaces for religion or nationality. In the second instance the registrar wrote in the space for nationality "Father Jewish; mother non-Jewish." In the space for religion they wrote "not registered."

Shalit petitioned the High Court of Justice, demanding that the nationality of his children be registered as Jews, and, since both he and his wife regarded themselves as atheists, that in the space for religion the children be registered as "no religion." Initially, the High Court recommended to the government that it eliminate the law requiring a citizen to enter his nationality and suggested that only citizenship and religion be stated. But the government, concerned about the internal security problems of Arab citizens of Israel, rejected the Court's recommendation. The Court had no choice but to render a judgment.

After a historic debate in the Israeli Knesset (parliament), the Court ruled that the registrar had to register the children as Jewish by nationality, even though their mother was not Jewish.

The decision caused a furor in Orthodox circles. There

was fear that the decision would be interpreted as sanction-
ing intermarriage in Israel and abroad. After a historic debate
in the Knesset an amendment to the Law of Return was
enacted in 1970, which for the first time accepted the halakhic
definition: "A Jew is a person born to a Jewish mother or who
has converted to Judaism and is not a member of another
religion."

The last phrase was intended to ensure that people like
Brother Daniel could not be considered Jewish for the purpose of the Law of Return.

8. Here are some textual sources related to who is a Jew.
You may wish to use them in your deliberations for the case
of Brother Daniel.

   (a) Jew: 1. An adherent of Judaism 2. A descendant of
   the Hebrew people. (Definition taken from the
   American Heritage Dictionary of the English Language.)
   (b) Judaism is a way of life. Its test of a man is not
   what he believes but how he lives, what he does, how
   he treats his fellow man. . . . Judaism rejects passing
   the buck to God. Judaism lays stress on social justice.
   . . . Judaism is a call to moral action. (Albert Vorspan)
   (c) Our people is only a people by virtue of its teachings. (Saadiah Gaon)
   (d) Why are we Jews? How strange this question is.
   Inquire of the fire why it burns? Ask the sun why it
   shines. Ask of the tree why it grows. Similarly, ask the
   Jew why he is Jewish. We are incapable of being other
   than what we are. That which is against us is within
   our very being, a manifestation of our soul, part of our
   heart. It cannot be nullified or vanquished. (Achad
   Ha-am)
   (e) The Jew is one whom other men consider a Jew.

That is the simple truth from which we must start. It is neither their past, their religion, nor their soil that unites the sons of Israel. If they have a common bond, if all of them deserve the name of a Jew ... that is, they live in a community which takes them for Jews. (Jean Paul Sartre)

(f) A Jew is anyone who says he is. (David Ben-Gurion)

DEBRIEFING

The final part of every simulation is called the debriefing session. When the debate has concluded, it is time to give participants a chance to express how they feel and what they have learned. The first thing to be done in the debriefing is to have the participants drop the roles they have been playing. Two kinds of initial questions ought to be encouraged. Questions such as "what happened?" and "how do you feel?" are good beginning ones. The next important question is "what did you learn?"

Following are some additional questions that you may wish to discuss and try to answer during the debriefing session.

Questions to Think About

After the debriefing of the case, here are some additional questions to discuss with your teacher and classmates.

1. Do you have to be religious to be Jewish?
2. Do you have to feel Jewish to be Jewish?
3. Do you have to be born Jewish to be Jewish?
4. If you convert out of Judaism, can you still be considered a Jew?

5. If you do not convert out of Judaism but do not want to be associated with anything Jewish, should you still be considered Jewish?

6. Who should determine whether someone is to be considered a Jew?

7. Is it more important to consider yourself Jewish or for others to consider you Jewish?

8. According to Jewish law and tradition, children born of Jewish fathers and non-Jewish mothers are not Jews and must convert if they wish to claim their father's faith. In 1984, the Reform Movement made a contribution to the issue of who is a Jew. It was debated whether a child born of a Jewish father and a non-Jewish mother could be considered Jewish if they raised the child with a Jewish identity. In a resolution then passed by a three-to-one margin, the Central Conference of American Rabbis agreed to recognize children with one Jewish parent of either sex as Jews if they rear the child as a Jew and identify formally and publicly with the Jewish faith. What in your opinion are the pros and cons of this decision? How did this complicate the discussion of who is a Jew?

9. Mrs. Pagano was born in Nebraska of a Jewish mother and a Methodist father. As a youth she rarely went to synagogue. She was not confirmed, and she married a Methodist and now has three children of her own. She has nothing to do with the synagogue. She no longer celebrates the Jewish holidays. Is Mrs. Pagano a Jew? Are Mrs. Pagano's children Jews? Why or why not?

10. Many Jewish scholars agree that the tradition behind matrilineal descent (i.e., a child born of a Jewish mother is Jewish) is derived from historical experience rather than divine command. The idea became current during the Roman occupation of Palestine when Jewish women were

forcibly or otherwise impregnated by soldiers, according to Rabbi Seymour Siegel of the Conservative Movement. The goal was to keep these women and children in the Jewish community by saying that the child would follow the mother's religion. The tradition continued, Rabbi Siegel stated, and we do not change tradition without a compelling reason. Are there compelling reasons to change the tradition of matrilineal descent?

11. Moishe Rosen is a born Jew who founded the controversial Jews for Jesus movement. He describes himself as a Jew who believes that Jesus is the Messiah. He has often said that because he believes in Jesus his intelligence has been impugned by rabbis and other Jewish community leaders. Would you consider Moishe Rosen Jewish? Why or why not?

12. In the early 1970s, a man named Marcus Shloimovitz lost his long fight to force the *Oxford English Dictionary* to eliminate what he considered defamatory definitions of the word "Jew." Over many years Shloimovitz pressured numerous publishers of other dictionaries to revise their definitions. With regard to the *Oxford English Dictionary* he was objecting to the secondary definition of a Jew as "a grasping or extortionate moneylender or usurer, or a trader who drives hard bargains or deals craftily." Arguing his case before the court he said that such anti-Semitic definitions were a slow poison of hatred in our midst and that such a definition defamed Jews. Should a dictionary have the right to print any definition of a word that it wishes to? Why or why not? What do you think is a good definition of the word "Jew" that most people could accept?

13. In the early 1990s, two spectacular airlifts brought more than 21,000 Ethiopians to Israel. These Ethiopians had

continued to nurture their Jewishness under difficult circumstances. Doubts were raised about their Jewishness by the Orthodox Israeli rabbinate, and in 1984 the Ethiopians found their circumcision rites challenged. Furthermore, the Ethiopian spiritual leaders, known as *kessim*, who had presided over marriages, divorces, circumcisions, and funerals in Ethiopia, wanted to be able preside in Israel. Israel's chief rabbi said not until they studied relevant Jewish law and passed a certification exam. The problem, of course, is that Ethiopian Jewish tradition only includes the Torah. The Talmud and other later commentaries never came their way. How would you rule on the Jewishness of the Ethiopians? Would you allow their spiritual leaders to perform life-cycle events in Israel?

14. What makes one a Jew? When all is said and done, who should be considered a Jew?

2

The Disputation of Tortosa

February 1413 (The case continued until November 12, 1414, and lasted over 69 sessions.)
Tortosa, Spain

BACKGROUND

The point of this debate was to settle the question of the relative merits of Judaism and Christianity. The order for the Jewish representatives to participate in this debate was issued by Benedict XIII. Benedict was an anti-pope (i.e., most Christians did not consider him the legitimate pope). Only Spain recognized his papal authority. Consequently, he thought he would add to his reputation by focusing the eyes of Christians on an attempt he would conduct to refute Judaism. The disputers were the ex-Jew Joshua Lorki, who opened for the Christians, and Vidal Benveniste, who opened for the Jews.

Benedict presided, and made it plain to the twenty-two Jewish representatives that the truth of Christianity was above contention and that the truth of Judaism was admitted up until the time of the rise of Christianity. The Jews were merely to answer whether or not certain passages of the Talmud bore witness to the fact that the Messiah had come before the destruction of the Temple. The apostate Lorki chose for the text of his sermon the words of Isaiah: "If you be willing and obedient, you shall eat the good of the land. But if you refuse and rebel, you shall be eaten by the sword." He also denigrated the Talmud as a damaging work which should be done away with.

The Jewish spokesman, Benveniste, answered with a long discourse in Latin.

DECISION
Benedict issued a statement forbidding Jews to study the Talmud, read anti-Christian writings, have sexual relations with Christians, and disinherit baptized children. Jews were denied all rights of internal jurisdiction. They could hold no public office and were forced to listen to Christian sermons in their synagogues. Many Jews converted to Christianity.

DEBATE
The class will now have an opportunity to reenact and debate some of the identical issues in the Tortosa dispute.

Participants will include Joshua Lorki and his assistants, who will debate the merits of Jesus as the Messiah. The opposing team will consist of Vidal Beneviste and his assistants, who will try to prove that Jesus could not possibly be the Messiah. The remainder of the students, along with the teacher, may serve as judges.

Fast Facts
Following are some fast facts to help each of the sides begin to prepare their case. Once they have done so the teacher can set forth the ground rules for the debate. (Note: It is suggested that each participant speak for no more than a couple of minutes and that time be allowed for questions and rebuttal.)

1. The Word Messiah: Messiah in Hebrew is *moshiach*, meaning "anointed one." Originally the term was a reference

to the high priest, who had oil poured on his head when he was consecrated to his spiritual office. In 1 Samuel 24:7, the king of Israel was called *moshiach Adonai*, the "anointed of God." The Messiah thus came to mean one to whom God delegated regal responsibility.

2. In some of the prophetic biblical books—Isaiah, Micah, Jeremiah, and Zechariah—there is described an ideal future leader who will rule over Israel in the "end of days," an age of redemption. Although this leader is not called the Messiah, it appears to be referring to one.

3. The ideal future leader was envisioned as a human being, a Jew descended from the House of David, of the seed of Jesse, a man of lofty moral and spiritual quality, wise, understanding, inspired, and courageous. This was the beginning of the Messiah and the messianic era.

4. This leader would be appointed by God and armed by God with authority. He will throw off the yoke of Israel's oppressors and reestablish the land of Israel.

5. According to the prophets, when this leader arrives every man will dwell under his fig tree unafraid. Justice will well up like a mighty stream and nation will not lift up sword against nation. Finally, the nations will come to the House of God and all will worship the one God.

6. Jewish tradition described Elijah the Prophet as the forerunner of the Messiah.

7. According to the *Shulchan Arukh* (Melachim 12:2), in the days of the Messiah there will be no hunger or war, no jealousy or strife. Prosperity will be universal and the world's predominant occupation will be "to know God."

8. Jewish tradition teaches that after the coming of the Messiah, all the dead will be resurrected and will be judged by God for what they did in their lives.

CHRISTIANITY AND JESUS THE MESSIAH

1. The interpretation of Jesus set forth by the apostle Paul and still later by the Greek fathers of the Church included the belief that Jesus was the son of God. He became God who assumed the flesh of man in order to die for and thereby expiate the sins of people. The word *Christ* is from the Greek and means Messiah.

2. According to Christianity, Jesus the Messiah is both savior and redeemer.

3. Jesus is the son of God born of a human mother. He will bring redemption to the individual soul.

4. Without belief in Jesus as the savior, Christianity collapses.

5. According to many Christian interpreters, the "he" in Isaiah 53:12 ("yet he bore the sin of many") is a reference to the Messiah who died. (According to Jewish interpretation, the reference is to the collective persecuted people of Israel some 700 years before Jesus was born.)

6. The early Christians believed that Jesus was the Messiah foretold by the prophets. Here are some verses from the Bible that are often used by Christians as proof of Jesus as the Messiah:

> Behold the days come, says God, that I will make a new covenant with the house of Israel. . . . And they shall no more teach every man his neighbor saying, "Know God," for they shall all know me. For I will forgive their iniquity, and I will remember their sin no more.
>
> (Jeremiah 31:31–34)

I will fill the House of David and the dwellers of Jerusalem with a spirit of pity and compassion, and they shall lament about me those whom they have pierced.

(Zechariah 12:10)

He is despised and rejected of men. He was wounded for our transgressions and he was bruised for our sins. And with his stripes we are healed.

(Isaiah 53:3–5)

God will raise up unto you a prophet from the midst of you, of your brethren, like unto me. Unto him you shall listen. I will raise up a prophet from among the brethren, like unto you, and will put my words in his mouth.

(Deuteronomy 18:15,18)

Your king is coming, yet humble, on a donkey.

(Zechariah 9:9)

For unto us a child is born, a son is given. And the government shall be upon his shoulder, and his name shall be called Wonderful, Counsellor, the Mighty God, the Everlasting Father, the Prince of Peace.

(Isaiah 9:6)

8. In Christian thought redemption means redemption from sin through belief in Jesus.

DEBRIEFING
Participants in the debate are mainly judged on the creativeness of their arguments. After the winner is declared, it is wise to offer participants a chance to discuss their feelings and what they have learned in the debate.

Questions to Think About
1. Do you believe in a personal Messiah?
2. How will you know when the Messiah comes?
3. What should Jews believe about Jesus?
4. Do you believe that there will ever be a time when the prophet Isaiah's prediction that "nation shall no more lay sword against nation" will come true?
5. According to the Talmud (Shabbat 118b), "the Messiah will come when the entire Jewish people observe two Sabbaths in succession." What do you think this really means? Is it possible?
6. Throughout Jewish history many people have claimed to be the Messiah. They are called "false Messiahs." Shabbetai Tzevi in 1648 was one of the most notorious. Who are some of the false Messiahs of today?
7. Some Jews, generally those affiliated with the Reform and Reconstructionist movements, believe that the messianic era will be ushered in not by a single individual known as the Messiah but by the cumulative activities of the entire Jewish people. What do you believe?
8. The last of Maimonides' Thirteen Principles of Faith is: "I believe with perfect faith in the coming of Messiah, and though Messiah may tarry, I will wait daily for his coming." Do you believe in this principle?

3

Baruch Spinoza

July 27, 1656
Amsterdam

BACKGROUND

After the expulsion of the Jews from Spain in 1492, thousands dispersed throughout the world. Many first settled in Portugal and later went to Holland. Soon the city of Amsterdam became a center of Jewish life in northern Europe.

Baruch Spinoza, a Dutch Jewish philosopher, was born in 1632 to parents of Portuguese Jewish background. He was sent to the school of the local Jewish community, where he excelled in his studies. Because he had a passion for philosophy, Spinoza began to raise issues which the Jewish community considered to be radical. The Jewish community of Amsterdam was outraged at Baruch Spinoza's so-called heretical views. These issues included the following:

1. He rejected ceremonial Judaism.
2. He insisted that religious tenets be judged only on the basis of reason.
3. He rejected Moses as the author of the Torah and the possibility of his being a genuine prophet.
4. He argued that since God determined nature within the

parameters of His law, nothing supernatural was possible.

5. He asserted that biblical moral teachings were simply those compatible with human reason.

6. He argued that God is not a purposeful divine being: God just is, and due to God's being everything happens of necessity. God does not act independently of the world, for God is the world. God is not the creator of the world because God and the world are synonymous.

7. God acts independently of the world, and the so-called "will of God" is nothing other than the workings of nature. Therefore, all events are the mechanical operation of natural-divine laws which function according to their predetermined pattern.

8. God is not a personal God. God does not have intellect or will, does not watch over people, does not know people, and is not a loving parent. To assume that God acts one way toward some people and differently toward others is sheer nonsense.

9. Free will is an illusion. People are not free to do what they want. Everything we do is conditioned by the circumstances that precede them, and these circumstances are determined by causes that precede them as well.

10. Bible stories are never to be believed literally, but rather are intended to instruct people, since we have difficulty understanding abstract concepts.

DECISION
In early 1656, Spinoza's heretical opinions began to attract the attention of the rabbinical council of Amsterdam. On July 27, Baruch Spinoza was excommunicated. The rabbinical pronouncement signed by Saul Levi Morteira and others states:

The chiefs of the council make known to you that having long known of evil opinions and acts of Baruch de Spinoza, they have endeavored by various means and promises to turn him from evil ways. Not being able to find any remedy, but on the contrary receiving every day more information about the abominable heresies practiced and taught by him, and about the monstrous acts committed by him, having this from many trustworthy witnesses who have deposed and borne witness on all this in the presence of said Spinoza, who has been convicted; all this having been examined in the presence of the rabbis, the council decided with the advice of the rabbis, that the said Spinoza should be excommunicated and cut off from the Nation of Israel.

Spinoza was then cursed, and everyone in the Jewish community was forbidden to be in contact with him. He accepted his excommunication with courage, saying, "It compels me to nothing which I should not have done in any case."

In 1660, Spinoza left Amsterdam and changed his name to Benedictus (the Latin equivalent of Baruch) and became involved with some liberal Protestants. He managed to live out his life without belonging to any sect or church.

Spinoza began to write down many of his ideas, although he was reluctant to publish them for fear of further harassment.

There have been many attempts to revoke the edict of the excommunication of Spinoza. Israeli Prime Minister David Ben-Gurion urged that the excommunication ban be lifted. However, the religious leaders of Amsterdam, the only group who have the official power to lift a ban initiated in their own city, have not responded favorably, perhaps because they believe that today's rabbinate lacks the authority to void a decree of this kind.

DEBATE

The class will now have an opportunity to reenact and debate some of the same issues that Spinoza faced in Amsterdam before the Jewish council. Participants will include Spinoza and his attorney and assistants, and the chiefs of the council, including Saul Levi Morteira. The chiefs of the council will attempt to prove that Spinoza's beliefs are so heretical that they endanger the lives of the Jewish community. Spinoza will attempt to prove that his beliefs are consistent with Judaism and in no way a threat to Jewish existence. The remainder of students, along with the teacher, may choose to serve as judges.

Fast Facts

Following is a summary of Spinoza's so-called heretical beliefs about God and the Bible as compared to the traditional rabbinic views on these issues:

1. God's Nature

Rabbis: There are no systematic views concerning God and God's nature in rabbinic thought. However, there is some consensus. God exists, there is only one God, God has many names in the Bible, and the rabbis introduced many new names as well (e.g., *Harachaman*—the Merciful One; *Hamakom*—the Place; *Ribbono shel olam*—Master of the Universe; *Avinu shebashamayim*—Our Father in Heaven); God judges the world using His attributes of justice and mercy, God and the Jewish people are joined in an intimate covenantal relationship; God is a personal God, accessible to us through prayer; angels are God's messengers.

Spinoza: God and the universe are one. God is nature. The laws of nature were set by God, and everything follows their structure.

2. Basic Questions

Rabbis: God exists. How can we serve God?

Spinoza: What is God? How can we know God?

3. God's Unity

Rabbis: God is one and unique. Angels exist as God's messengers.

Spinoza: God is one. There is no dualism of mind and matter.

4. Knowing God

Rabbis: We cannot know God.

Spinoza: God is the totality of the universe. The more we know about the structure of the world, the more we know about God.

5. God's Name

Rabbis: God has many names, each describing a different attribute of God's personality.

Spinoza: No unique name.

6. God's Relationship in the World

Rabbis: God judges the world, rewarding the good and punishing evil.

Spinoza: The laws of nature are manifestations of God. God does not act independently of the world. God is the world.

7. God and the Jewish People
Rabbis: God gave the Jews both a Written and an Oral Torah at Sinai. God loves the Jews and chose them as a special people. The relationship is a covenantal one. God expects the Jews to fulfill those things that God wants of them. By doing those things (i.e., the mitzvot) the Jews show their love for God.
Spinoza: God has no special relationship with Israel or any other people. The laws of nature—God—operate equally for all.

8. What God Wants
Rabbis: God wants ethical behavior and observance of the mitzvot.
Spinoza: God wants nothing. God as nature simply is.

9. God and the Individual
Rabbis: God is a personal God who hears and answers the prayers of each individual.
Spinoza: God is not a personal God. God is the laws of nature, and the world is determined. Our only freedom comes through knowledge.

DEBRIEFING
After the winner is declared, it is essential to offer all participants a chance to discuss their feelings and the things that were learned and argued during the debate.

Questions to Think About
1. Is it proper for all people, like Spinoza, to each find the meaning of God in their own way, through the searching of their own minds?

2. Is it important to know and follow the teachings of the rabbis vis-à-vis their understanding of God?

3. Here are some God concepts as they appear in the prayerbook. To which ones do you subscribe:

(a) God is One.

(b) God listens to prayer.

(c) God accepts true repentance.

(d) God is eternal.

(e) God has no form.

(f) God knows a person's innermost thoughts.

(g) God loves Israel.

(h) God has chosen Israel.

(i) God rewards and punishes in a just manner.

(j) God will resurrect the dead.

(k) God is dependable.

(l) God brings miracles.

4. Are there any of Spinoza's views to which you subscribe?

5. What makes a belief heretical to Judaism? Do you think that Spinoza should have been excommunicated for his beliefs?

6. Spinoza has been described as "the most impious atheist that ever lived upon the face of the earth." On the other hand, he has also been called a "God-intoxicated man." What is your opinion of these quotations? What do you think they mean?

7. For Spinoza, to know God means to understand, as much as one is capable, the relationship between parts of the world and in particular to know our place in the universe. What do you think Spinoza means? What is our place in the universe?

8. Spinoza wrote in his *Ethics* that "the human mind can-

not be absolutely destroyed with the body, but there remains of it something which is eternal." Do you agree with this statement?

9. The noted historian Arthur Hertzberg has described Spinoza as the first modern Jew because he was the first to leave the Jewish community without becoming a Christian. Do you agree with this statement? How would you define a modern Jew?

10. In your estimation was Baruch Spinoza a Jew?

4

The Dreyfus Affair

1894–1899
France

BACKGROUND

Alfred Dreyfus was an officer in the French army. In 1892, he became a captain on the general staff, where he was the only Jew. In the fall of 1894, a secret military document, known as a *bordereau*, sent by a French officer to the military attaché of the German embassy in Paris fell into the hands of the French intelligence service. On the basis of a similarity in handwriting and anti-Jewish prejudice, the heads of the intelligence service suspected Dreyfus. He was arrested and tried before a court-martial.

The case began late in the year and lasted four days. Seven judges composed the court. Besides the judges there remained in the courtroom only Dreyfus and his attorney, the prefect of police, and Colonel Georges Picquart.

Dreyfus was unanimously pronounced guilty . His sentence was life imprisonment in a fortress, preceded by military degradation. He was then exiled to Devil's Island, where he was confined in a small hut.

On January 13, 1898, the newspaper *L'Aurore* published an open letter from the novelist Émile Zola to the president of the French Republic entitled "J'accuse," which accused the denouncers of Dreyfus of malicious libel. The article made a powerful impression. Two hundred thousand copies were sold in Paris. Zola was found guilty of libel. Officers of the general staff threatened to resign if Dreyfus was acquitted. Anti-Semitic riots occurred in different parts of the country.

A second trial took place in 1899, and the court-martial decided by a majority that Dreyfus had committed treason—but because of "extenuating circumstances," he was sentenced to only ten years' imprisonment, five of which he had already served.

In 1904, with a leftist government newly established, Dreyfus demanded a fresh investigation. The Court of Appeals reexamined the case and in 1906 pronounced that the evidence against Dreyfus was completely unsubstantiated and that it was unnecessary to order a further trial to exonerate him.

Interestingly, the Dreyfus trial turned Theodor Herzl, father of the Jewish state, toward the Zionist solution. What particularly struck him were the cries of the frenzied French mobs at the public ceremony of Dreyfus's humiliation. In addition to calling for the death of Dreyfus, they also called for the death of all Jews. Herzl concluded that as long as Jews lived in non-Jewish societies, they would continually be collectively blamed and hated for the wrongful actions of any of them. If "Death to the Jews" was the reaction in liberal France, the first European country to grant the Jews equal rights, it meant that Jews were not safe except in a land of their own. In 1897, Herzl convened the First Zionist Congress in Basle, Switzerland.

Fast Facts

Following is an alphabetized annotated list of characters in the Dreyfus affair that you may wish to have appear at the mock-trial.

Bastian, Marie Agent for the statistical section, employed in the German embassy. Her cover job as a cleaning woman enabled her to search the garbage bags and hand over scraps of paper and fragments.

Bertillon, Alphonse Chief of the identification department of the judicial police. He testified at the 1894 trial and at Rennes that the *bordereau* was in Dreyfus's handwriting.

Billot, General Jean Baptiste Lifetime senator and minister of war, he remained convinced of Dreyfuss' guilt.

Boisdeffre, General Raoul François Charles Le Mouton de Army chief of staff from 1893 to 1898. He remained convinced that Dreyfus's guilt was a certainty.

Demange, Edgar Lawyer for Alfred Dreyfus at 1894 court-martial.

Dreyfus, Captain Alfred Probationer on the general staff when he was accused of passing military secrets to the Germans.

Dreyfus, Lucie Wife of Alfred Dreyfus.

Drumont, Edouard Anti-Semitic leader, he attacked Jewish bankers in particular and Jews in general.

Du Paty de Clam, Major Mercier General staff officer. In 1894, after Dreyfus's arrest, he was the first to declare that the *bordereau* was in Dreyfus's hand and testified against him at the trial.

Esterhazy, Ferdinand Walsin Infantry officer, he spent his whole life gambling, amassing debts, and running after women. In 1894, he approached German attaché

Schwartzkoppen and began to spy for him. He was the true author of the *bordereau* for which Dreyfus was convicted. When suspicion began to focus on him he attempted to save himself from a court-martial by inventing a veiled lady, claiming that she had sent him a photograph of a document given to her by Picquart. Esterhazy was acquitted.

Gonse, General Charles Arthur Deputy chief of staff, he gave evidence at 1894 trial that the *bordereau* was in Dreyfus's writing.

Henry, Major Hubert Joseph Member of the statistical section, he testified at the first trial that Dreyfus was a traitor.

Jouaust, Colonel Albert The presiding judge at the court-martial at Rennes in 1899.

Labori, Ferdinand Distinguished criminal lawyer, known for his flamboyant manner, he defended Zola as well as Dreyfus at the Rennes trial.

Loubet, Émile President of the French Republic, he pardoned Dreyfus.

Mercier, General Auguste Responsible for the arrest of Dreyfus in 1894, remained an accomplice to the injustices done to Dreyfus.

Picquart, Major Georges He was present at the court-martial of Dreyfus in 1894 and later became head of the statistical section. In 1896, he came into the possession of fragments of a letter known as *le petit bleu* addressed to Major Esterhazy. Later he discovered that the writing of the *bordereau* was in Esterhazy's hand. Convinced that Dreyfus was innocent he went to his superior officers who were unwilling to reopen the Dreyfus case. Picquart was sent to prison and dismissed from the army.

Saussier, General Felix Gaston As military governor of Paris, he recommended against pursuing the investigation of Dreyfus but was finally forced to order the court-martial.

Schwartzkoppen, Colonel Max von Military attaché in the German embassy in Paris, he conducted espionage operations. He employed Esterhazy as a spy from 1894 to 1896. He denied repeatedly that he had any dealings with Dreyfus.

Zola, Émile French novelist and champion of Alfred Dreyfus. His involvement reached a climax with the publication of his article "J'accuse." For this he was tried and found guilty of libel, but the verdict was overturned by the Court of Appeals. During a second trial in Versailles he fled to England to avoid his sentence.

Questions to Think About

1. At the time of the eruption of the Dreyfus affair France's Jewish population was no more than 75,000, but the concentration of 40,000 Jews in Paris, site of the national press, made the Jewish population all the more visible. Many of the Parisian Jews were newcomers from the eastern provinces of Alsace-Lorraine, lost to Germany in the Franco-Prussian War, or from the Russian Empire. The former often spoke French with a strong German accent and the latter with a Yiddish accent. Some historians have said that this situation confirmed hostile observers in their belief that all Jews in France were foreigners and hence could not be trusted. What do you think? Does being different raise issues of bias in a community?

2. When the Dreyfus affair first broke, French Jews were said to have maintained a discreet and quiet stance during

the early years. Although disturbed by Dreyfus's arrest and shouts of "Death to the Jews," they remained relatively passive. Why do you think this was so? If you had lived during this time, what do you think you would have done?

3. In 1895, the chief rabbi of France, Zadoc Kahn, privately convened a secret committee of defense against the anti-Semitism of the time. In 1902, when the existence of the committee was discovered, anti-Semites attacked it as another example of a Jewish conspiracy. This experience points to the quandary faced by the leaders of the organized Jewish community in attempting to find an effective response to anti-Semitism. On the one hand, their silence was taken for shame or admission of guilt or cowardice; their organized opposition as proof of a Jewish plot. What do you think would be your "game plan" if you experienced anti-Semitic crimes in your community? Is there ever a time when it would be right to take the law into your own hands?

4. What do you think causes people to hate?

5. It has been said by historians that the Dreyfus Affair inspired Theodor Herzl's Zionist principles? Can you think of other examples of a difficult time befalling the Jewish people that led to a positive response or action?

6. The Dreyfus Affair has engaged the minds and passions of artists and intellectuals as few other political scandals ever have. Why do you think there is still so much interest and fascination in the Dreyfus case?

7. What have you learned from the Dreyfus Affair that could be applied to modern-day political scandals? Have you encountered any scandal that is in any way similar to the Dreyfus Affair?

5

Jeremiah's Trial for Treason

600 B.C.E.
Temple Gate in Jerusalem

BACKGROUND

After the death of his father Josiah, King Jehoiakim was placed on the throne of Judah by the Egyptian pharaoh. Because of the tremendous political unrest both within and outside Judah, Jehoiakim feared open revolt at any moment. He called a council to determine what should be done with the prophet Jeremiah, who had preached what might well be labeled a treasonous sermon within the precincts of the Jerusalem Temple. A number of people wanted to put him to death on the spot, but King Jehoiakim called for a general hearing where all major parties might testify in relation to the case. These parties, the army, the priests, the Deuteronomic reformers, and Jeremiah himself, will determine his fate.

The situation for which Jeremiah is on trial is recorded in Jeremiah 26:1–15.

> In the beginning of the reign of Jehoiakim, the son of Josiah, king of Judah, came this word from God saying: Thus says God: Stand in the court of God's house, and speak to all the cities of Judah, which come to

worship in God's house, all the words that I command you to speak to them. Do not diminish even a single word. Perhaps they will listen and turn back, each of them for his evil way, that I may renounce the punishment I am planning to bring upon them for their wicked deeds. Say to them: "Thus says God: If you do not obey Me, following the teaching that I have given you, heeding the words of my servants the prophets whom I have been sending you, then I will make this House of Shiloh and I will make this city a curse for all the nations of the earth."

The priests and the prophets and all the people heard Jeremiah speaking these words in the House of God. And when Jeremiah finished speaking all that God had commanded him to speak to all the people, the priests and the prophets and all the people laid hold of him saying: "You shall surely die. How dare you prophesy in the name of God that this House shall become like Shiloh, and this city shall be desolate, without an inhabitant?" And all the people were gathered against Jeremiah in the house of God.

When the princes of Judah heard these things, they came up from the king's house to the house of God, and they sat in the entry of the new gate of God's house. Then the priests and the prophets spoke to the princes and all the people saying: "This man is worthy of death, for he has prophesied against this city, as you have heard with your ears." Then Jeremiah spoke to all the princes and to all the people saying: "God has sent me to prophesy against this house and against this city all the words that you have heard. Now, therefore, amend your ways and your doings, and listen to the voice of the Lord your God. And God will renounce the punishment that He has decreed for you. As for me, I am in your hands. Do to me what seems good and right to you. But know that if you put me to death, you and this city and its inhabitants will be guilty of shedding the blood of an innocent man. For in truth God has sent me to you, to speak all these words to you."

After reading the preceding Bible story, the class should be divided into four small groups:

The Deuteronomic scholars: Defenders of the Law.

The priests: Impassioned priests who see Jerusalem as the symbol of Israel and the national unity.

Army officers: A group of officers who see Jeremiah as a threat to the morale of the nation.

Baruch: Jeremiah's scribe and secretary, who believes that Jeremiah is a patriot and a true prophet.

Following is a more detailed description of each of these groups and the texts they will need to read to help them with their tasks.

Deuteronomic Scholars

This is a group of distinguished scholars who have worked tirelessly on the Law. This group is not sure about Jeremiah since his Temple sermon but have felt in the past that he supports a renewed faith and belief in Judah. This group will want to appoint Huldah and the scribe Hilkiah to be its representatives at the council of the king. The group's task will be to determine how to use its special interests and powers

in the decision-making process. It will want to read
Deuteronomy 13 and 18:9–22.

These scholars were responsible for the reforms of King
Josiah in 622 B.C.E. They have always felt that reform was
essential if Judah was to survive as a nation, especially after
the dreadful King Manasseh who preceded King Josiah.
However, the group questions whether or not Jeremiah constitutes a real threat to the nation since he may now be going
beyond reform, seeming to be announcing God's unconditional judgment of Judah. The group is reluctant to banish
any prophet who claims to be speaking to God, and looks to
guidelines in Deuteronomy 13 and 18:9–20 for determining
who is a true prophet and who is not.

Priests

These are the fervent priests of Jerusalem who see in
Jeremiah a threat to the national ideology that Jerusalem cannot be conquered by force. Jeremiah's attack on the Temple
in his speech in chapter 26 constitutes a violation of the official theology which has been in existence since the days of
King David. This group will want to appoint the priest
Zadok and the priestess Baalita to be its representatives at
the council of the king. It will be their task to determine how
to use its special interests and powers in the decision-making
process. Suggested passages to read in preparation for the
council are Isaiah 2:1–4 and 2 Kings 18–19.

Their ancestry dates from the time of Zadok, the first
priest appointed by Kind David in Jerusalem. They believe
that Zion is the sign of God's rule on earth. To proclaim, as
Jeremiah does, that the Temple can be destroyed is the same
as saying "God is dead." This group believes that they must
protect the official theology at all costs. The God of history is

on the side of the Jews. Therefore, they feel that Jeremiah should be silenced and banished from the state of Judah, since he has profaned God's Holy Name.

The Army

This group sees Jeremiah as a direct threat to the already sagging morale of the nation. His sermon, they feel, constitutes an act of treason since Jerusalem is close to a state of war. The group will thus wish to appoint a captain and a general to represent its view at the council. It will also want to read Joshua 6 and Exodus 15.

The army believes that since the time of the exodus from Egypt, God has continually defeated Israel's enemies in times of national crisis. Although the idea of the holy war had been pushed into the background in recent times, it favors the reinstitution of the holy war under King Josiah. The army believes that God will fight for Israel against the Babylonians and give them victory as God did against the Assyrians a century before. Therefore, the real issue is to encourage the people to believe in God's deliverance, which will destroy the enemy. Jeremiah undermines this faith because he feels that the nation can no longer rely on God to deliver her because she has sinned and must expect the judgment of God. He speaks an untruth and therefore must be excommunicated from public life.

Baruch and Jeremiah

This group is a party of two. Baruch, Jeremiah's secretary, wholeheartedly believes that Jeremiah is a faithful supporter of the nation. (For background data you may want to read Jeremiah 7 and 26:27–28.) Jeremiah is a real patriot who is simply interpreting the covenant that God has established with Judah. Jeremiah is a true prophet, not a traitor. Jeremiah is a prophet who simply is calling the people to new obedience while accepting the impending judgment of God. (To understand Baruch and his relationship to Jeremiah, you will find reading chapters 36 and 45 of Jeremiah very helpful.)

DEBATE

The trial will be chaired by the king, who will be recognized as the absolute authority in the kingdom of Judah. Each group will be allowed two representatives at the debate and allotted several minutes to state their case. Under the direction of the king, the assembled groups will try to present their case while answering these questions: Is Jeremiah guilty of treason and on what grounds? If Jeremiah is guilty, what ought to be his punishment? If Jeremiah is not guilty, should his activity in Jerusalem be curtailed?

Questions to Think About

1. If you were a prophet and God told you that it was useless for you to pray to God to intercede on behalf of the Jewish people, what would you do?

2. Can you think of other times in Jewish history when God seemed to forsake the Israelite people?

3. In chapter 26 of Jeremiah what finally convinces the people not to put Jeremiah to death for his speech of doom? (Hint: See verses 15–19.)

4. What is the moral of the Jeremiah story? In your estimation, is Jeremiah guilty of treason?

5. In the Bible, Jeremiah insists that national suffering comes as a punishment for national wrongdoing. What are the implications of this belief for an understanding of the fate of the Jews who suffered and died in the Holocaust?

6

The Trial of the Ten Spies

1300 B.C.E.
Canaan

BACKGROUND

Moses appoints a delegation of twelve Israelites, leaders of
each of the tribes of Israel, to go into Canaan and scout the
land. Ten spies return terrified. Years of Egyptian slavery
have ruined their self-confidence. They tell their fellow
Israelites that the Canaanites are so tall that "we were as
grasshoppers in their eyes." Although some of their report is
positive, they warn that it would be suicidal for the Israelites
to try to take over the land, for the Canaanites would surely
massacre them. Two spies, Caleb and Joshua, oppose the
report of their ten colleagues, assuring the people that there
is nothing to fear and that God is on their side.
Unfortunately, they are able to convince no one, including
the members of their own tribe. After accepting the majority
report, the people turn on Moses in fury: "Did you bring us
into the desert to die?" God is now very angry and decides
that the Israelites will now have to wander in the desert until
the entire generation that left Egypt dies out. God wants
Canaan to be occupied by a new generation conceived in
freedom and devoid of any slave mentality. Of all of the
Israelites who left Egypt with Moses, only two will be

allowed to enter Canaan: Joshua, who will become the successor to Moses, and Caleb.

The story (Numbers 13–14) should be carefully reviewed by all the participants before the trial begins.

> 1. God spoke to Moses: 2. "Send men that they may scout the land of Canaan which I am giving to the Israelite people. Send one man from each of their ancestral tribes . . ." 17. When Moses sent them to scout the land of Canaan, he said to them: "Go up there to the Negev and to the hill country. 18. See what kind of country it is. Are the people who live there strong or weak, few or many? 19. Is the country in which they dwell strong or weak? Is the country in which they live good or bad? Are the towns they live in open or fortified? 20. Is the soil rich or poor? Is it wooded or not? And take pains to bring back some of the fruit of the land . . ." 25. At the end of forty days they returned from scouting the land. 26. They went directly to Moses and Aaron and the whole Israelite community at Kadesh in the wilderness of Paran, and they gave their report to them and to the entire community, as they showed them the fruit of the land. 27. This is what they told him: "We came to the land to which you sent us; it does indeed flow with milk and honey, and this is its fruit. 28. But the people who inhabit the land are powerful, and the cities are fortified and very large. 29. Moreover, we saw the Anakites there. Amalekites dwell in the Negev region; Hittites, Jebusites, and Amorites live in the hill country. And Canaanites dwell by the Sea and along the Jordan." 30. Caleb quieted the people before Moses

and said: "Let's by all means go up and gain possession of the land, for we shall certainly overcome it."
31. But the men who had gone up with him said: "We
cannot attack that people, for it is stronger than we."
32. Thus they spread calumnies among the Israelites
about the land that they scouted, saying, "The country that we traversed and scouted is one that devours
its settlers. All the people that we saw in it are giants.
33. We saw the Nephilim there—the Anakites are part
of the Nephilim, and we looked like grasshoppers to
ourselves, and so we must have looked to them."

Chapter 14: 1. The whole community broke into loud
cries and the people cried all night. 2. All the Israelites
complained to Moses: "If only we had died in Egypt,"
the whole community shouted at them, "or if only we
might die in this wilderness. 3. Why is God taking us
to that land to fall by the sword . . ." 4. And they said
to one another: "Let us go back to Egypt." 5. Then
Moses and Aaron fell on their faces before all the
Israelites. 6. And Joshua son of Nun and Caleb son of
Jephunneh, of those who had scouted the land, rent
their clothing and 7. admonished the whole Israelite
community saying: "The land that we traversed and
scouted is a very good land. 8. If God is pleased with
us, God will bring us into that land, a land flowing
with milk and honey and give it to us. 9. Only you
must not rebel against God. Have no fear of the people of the country, for they are our prey. Their protec-
tion has departed from them, but God is with us. Be
not afraid of them." 10. As the whole community
threatened to throw stones at them, God appeared in

the Tent of Meeting to all of the Israelites. 11. God said to Moses: "How long will this people spurn Me, and how long will they have no faith in Me despite all the signs that I have given them? 12. I will strike you with pestilence . . ." 26. God further spoke to Moses and Aaron: "How much longer shall that wicked community keep muttering against Me . . . 30. Not one shall enter the land in which I swore to settle you, except for Caleb son of Jephunneh and Joshua son of Nun . . ." 36. As for the men who Moses sent to spy out the land, who came back and caused the whole community to mutter against him by spreading lies about the land, 37. those who spread such lies about the land died of plague, by the will of God. 38. Of those men who had gone to scout the land, only Joshua son of Nun and Caleb son of Jephunneh survived.

DEBATE

A trial will be staged in order to determine the guilt or innocence of the ten spies who brought back a negative report. The following are the spies who brought back a negative report:

Shammua, from the tribe of Reuben
Shaphat, from the tribe of Simeon
Igal, from the tribe of Issachar
Palti, from the tribe of Benjamin
Gaddiel, from the tribe of Zebulun
Manasseh, from the tribe of Joseph
Ammiel, from the tribe of Dan
Sethur, from the tribe of Asher

Nachbi, from the tribe of Naphtali

Geuel, from the tribe of Gad

The two spies who brought back the positive report are:

Caleb, from the tribe of Judah

Hosea, from the tribe of Ephraim (Moses changed Hosea's name to Joshua)

A judge and several judicial advisors should be selected from the class to try the case, and a prosecuting attorney representing God, and a defense attorney representing the ten spies who brought back a negative report ought to be selected in advance as well. Other participants who might be called to the stand include Moses and perhaps a member or two of the Israelite community who heard the report of the spies.

The judge will afford time for the prosecuting attorney to present the case against the spies. The defense attorney will have an opportunity to call witnesses (the ten spies) as well as to interrogate Caleb and Hosea.

After an agreed-upon time, the judge (along with the advisors) will have a chance to rule on the case, deciding whether the ten spies are to be found guilty because of their negative, demoralizing report, or not guilty.

DEBRIEFING

An opportunity for the teacher to debrief by allowing all the participants to share their observations with the whole group will then take place. The whole group works to summarize what has been learned, with the teacher acting as facilitator and moderator.

Questions to Think About

1. Following are several opinions of commentators regarding the sin of the spies. After reading them decide if any match your thoughts:

(a) Aaron Wildvasky: In his study *Moses as a Political Leader*, Wildavsky suggests that the sin of the spies is more serious than the heinous sin of slander. The Israelites have left Egypt with the promise of conquering the Land of Israel, which is their goal. The spies return and take advantage of the people's anticipation of their report to discredit the entire enterprise. That is their sin—one of conspiring to convince the people that God is leading them to disaster. Thus they essentially kill the hopes of their people.

(b) Pinchus Peli: He asserts that the spies' sin is their conducting a demoralizing campaign, deliberately deceiving the people with lies about the land which they have just scouted.

(c) Seymour Essrog: He posits that people often tend to underestimate themselves and demean their importance as people. When the spies said that "all the people that we saw are men of great size and we looked like grasshoppers to ourselves," this was their transgression (i.e., not believing in themselves and the power of the people of Israel).

2. Why do you think that an all-knowing God would tell Moses to spend spies when God knew they would bring back a false report?

3. There are commentators who state that the sin of the spies was in the use of the word "but." "But," they said, "the people who live there are powerful and the cities are fortified and very large." Had they left out the word "but" the spies

would have stayed within the limits of a factual report. When they added the word "but" it was no longer a factual account. Rather, it was an attempt to sway public opinion. How do you react to this commentary? Do you agree or disagree with it?

4. In the Bible story Moses asks the spies to bring him clear and precise answers to these questions:

(a) see what the land is

(b) see whether the people are weak or strong

(c) see whether the land is good or bad

(d) see what the cities are like

(e) see whether the land is fat or lean, wooded or clear

Are there other questions that you would have added to this list? What are the important questions that you believe need to be answered when a person sets out to explore a place in which to make his or her home?

5. Our sages once said that "a lie, to succeed, must contain a grain of truth." How does this principle apply to our Bible story? To which specific verse can this principle be applied?

6. Do you feel that God's punishment of the Israelites was commensurate with the crime? What was the sin of the people of Israel? What, in your opinion, was the sin of the spies?

7. Do you think it is disloyal for a Jew to spread an "evil report" about the State of Israel?

8. Can you think of any modern-day examples of the necessity for a person to "fudge the truth" for a greater cause?

7

The Trial of Abraham ben Terach for Attempted Homicide of Isaac ben Abraham

1800 B.C.E.
Mount Moriah, Israel

BACKGROUND

The story of Abraham's call by God to sacrifice his beloved son Isaac is one of the most dramatic and frightening stories in the entire Torah. The rabbis titled the story *Akedat Yitzchak,* "the binding of Isaac for a sacrifice," and chose it for the Torah reading on the second day of Rosh Hashanah. Abraham is put to the ultimate test, being asked to kill his beloved son Isaac for no other reason than that God asks him to do so.

One of the central problems that Bible readers have with Abraham's behavior is that he appears to so easily acquiesce to God's command to kill his son. He does so in the story seemingly without hesitation, without asking any questions, and without consulting anyone in his family, including his wife Sarah.

This simulation was created by Dr. Leora Isaacs for her eighth-grade class on the Book of Genesis at Temple Sholom Hebrew High School in Bridgewater, New Jersey. It has been staged and field-tested numerous times

The moral question regarding Abraham's behavior is as follows: Should a person who hears God's voice asking him to do something that clearly appears against good judgment do it without question?

The brief biblical narrative leaves readers with a difficult dilemma. Judaism regards Abraham as the first patriarch and father of the Israelites. Yet every Jew, indeed every human being, knows that if he heard of a father setting out to offer his child as a sacrifice at God's request, he would want to see that person committed to an insane asylum. How then are modern Jews to relate to Abraham, whose actions seem immoral or insane? If Abraham were tried in a Jewish court of law for the attempted homicide of his son Isaac, might he be found guilty?

Students will have an opportunity to stage a mock trial in which Abraham, the defendant, is being tried for the attempted murder of his son.

Before beginning the trial, all participants should carefully read the story of the sacrifice of Isaac as it appears in Genesis 22. Following are the important verses in the story:

1. Some time later, God put Abraham to the test. God said to him: "Abraham," and he answered, "Here I am." 2. And God said: "Take your son, your favorite one, Isaac, the one who you love, and proceed to the land of Moriah, and offer him on one of the high places that I will show you." 3. So early the next morning Abraham saddled his donkey and took with him his two servants and his son Isaac. He split the wood for the burnt offering, and he set out for the place which God had told him. 4. On the third day, Abraham looked up and saw that place in the dis-

tance. 5. Then Abraham said to his servants, "You stay here with the donkey. The boy and I will go up there, and we will worship and return to you." 6. Abraham took the wood for the burnt offering and put it on his son Isaac. He took the firestone and the knife, and the two of them walked off together. 7. Then Isaac said to his father Abraham: "Father." And he answered, "Yes, my son." And he said: "Here are the firestone and the wood, but where is the sheep for the burnt offering?" 8. And Abraham said: "God will provide the sheep for the burnt offering, my son." And the two of them walked together. 9. They arrived at the place which God told him. There Abraham built an altar. He laid out the wood and bound his son Isaac. He laid him on the altar, on top of the wood. 10. Abraham picked up the knife to slay his son. 11. Then an angel of God called to him from heaven: "Abraham, Abraham." And he answered, "Here I am." 12. And he said: "Do not raise your hand against the boy, or do anything to harm him. For now I know that you fear God, since you have not withheld your son, your favored one, from me." 13. When Abraham looked up, his eye glanced upon a ram, caught in the bushes by its horn. So Abraham went and took the ram and offered it up as a burnt offering in place of his son. 14. And Abraham named that site *Adonai-yireh* whence the present saying, "On the mount of God there is a vision." 15. The angel of God called to Abraham a second time from heaven, 16. and said, "By Myself I swear, God declares: `Because you have done this and have not withheld your son, your favored one, 17. I will bestow My blessing upon you and make your descendants as plentiful as the stars of heaven and the sands of the seashore, and your descendants shall seize the gates of their foes. 18. All the nations of the earth shall bless themselves by your descendants, because you have obeyed My command.'" 19. So Abraham returned to his servants, and they departed together for Beersheba, and Abraham stayed in Beersheba.

The following are additional incidents in the life of Abraham ben Terach which participants ought to include when preparing their case:

Abraham begins his relationship with God (Genesis 17).

Abraham moves to Canaan (Genesis 17).

Abraham's relationship with his nephew Lot, and the incident of land division (Genesis 13).

The move down to Egypt, and Abraham's representation of Sarah as his "sister" (Genesis 12).

Lot's kidnapping, and the allegiance of the four kings (Genesis 14).

The meeting with the three "strangers" (Genesis 17).

Abraham's argument with God on behalf of the righteous of Sodom (Genesis 18).

Abraham, Hagar, Sarah, and Ishmael (Genesis 21).

Abraham and his covenant(s) with God (Genesis 15, 17).

DEBATE

The attorneys for each "team" serve as team captains. They must coordinate their team's case, assist witnesses in their preparation, and be sure that all fulfil their responsibilities for the trial.

In addition, the attorneys for each team must prepare and deliver opening and closing remarks, and questions for cross-examining witnesses from the other team.

Each witness is part of a team, and therefore must assume responsibility and work cooperatively. Each witness is responsible for developing a list of questions for the attorneys that will help get their story across, and for being prepared to answer these questions as fully and dramatically as possible. Defense team witnesses should be sure to prepare questions that will show Abraham's actions and motivations in the best possible light. Prosecution team witnesses should do the opposite.

In addition, each witness should be prepared to respond to cross-examination from the opposing team. Try to "psych out" your opponents, guessing how they will try to turn your answers to their advantage. Be prepared to counter their strategies. (You will probably want to work as a team on this part of the assignment.)

Make sure all assertions are factually correct. You may refer to the biblical text, Midrash, and other commentaries as well as archaeological evidence. (Of course, top-notch lawyers will draw attention to what is in the Bible and what is Midrash in opposing testimony—and may raise objections when appropriate. At the same time, they will try to use any materials to their own advantage.)

Props, costumes, and the like are welcome, but will not replace poor preparation.

The defense team consists of Attorney 1, Abraham ben Terach, Lot, the Angel who brought the message about Sodom, the Angel that brought the message about Isaac's birth, the representative of the four kings, and the Angel who prevented the sacrifice.

The prosecution team consists of Attorney 2, Isaac, Sarah, Hagar, Ishmael, a servant, Pharaoh, the ram (eyewitness), and another servant.

The parents of the students in the class are sent jury notices, since they will be acting as the jury in the trial. Following is a sample letter.

Notice of Jury Duty

As many of you know, the eighth-graders have been studying the biblical narratives related to the patriarch Abraham. As a culminating activity to this unit of study, the class will be conducting a simulated trial, each student taking the role of an attorney, defendant, or witness. The students have been working very hard, and we know you will be very proud of their final results. Students will be evaluated on their preparation and participation in this learning activity.

To provide a jury for this trial, as well as an opportunity for parents to participate in their children's Jewish studies, the parents are hereby called for jury duty. You are respectfully requested to appear in court chambers [specify the location] on [specify date and time]. Abraham ben Terach will be tried for attempted homicide of his son Isaac. The trial will run for the first two periods (approximately one and a half hours)

Please return the attached response slip with your student, indicating whether you will be able to attend. We look forward to your joining with us. Thank you in advance for your interest and support.

(For further explanation, ask your eighth-grader! If you wish to prepare in advance, please review Genesis 12–22.)

Jury Duty Response Slip
(Please select one response)
I _____ will be able to report for jury duty.

I _____ respectfully request a deferral of jury duty, due to personal commitments.

Questions to Think About

1. Moses Maimonides asserts that the purpose of the so-called test of Abraham was to teach us how far one needs to go in order to show fear of God. He bases his reasoning on the verse "For now I know that you fear God, since you have not withheld your favorite son from me" (Genesis 22:12). What are your thoughts on Maimonides's assertion?

2. Lippman Bodoff asserts that the story of the sacrifice of Isaac was an attempt by Abraham to test God and ultimately test himself. That is to say, Abraham all along wanted to see if God would stop him, so Abraham used the strategy of stalling for time (e.g., Abraham gets up, he dresses his animals, then he gets his retinue in order, then he cuts firewood, and then he sets off. Each of these are separate steps intended to stall for time). By stalling for time Abraham tried to give God time to change His mind. What's your opinion of Bodoff's assertion? How does his assertion relate to whether or not Abraham should be found guilty for attempted homicide?

3. If you were Abraham and did not know what God truly had in mind in terms of the ultimate sacrifice of your son, would you have acted in a similar fashion? Is this the kind of loyalty that God demands of each and every one of us?

4. Is the story of the sacrifice of Isaac what true faith is really all about?

5. Are there things that you would have expected Abraham to do in the story? If yes, what are they?

6. Do you think that Abraham would have really gone through with the sacrifice of his son Isaac had the angel not stopped him? Prove it from the text.

7. What is the purpose of the servants in the story? Why do you think Abraham takes them along with him, and why does he leave them by themselves along the way?

8. Why do you think that God uses angels rather than His own voice in order to stop Abraham from killing his son? Why does God need to use two angels?

9. According to several rabbinic commentators, Abraham had questions and doubts about what God had commanded him to do. Find examples of Abraham's doubts.

10. As Jews, should we follow the commandments of our faith without ever questioning them? Are we disloyal if we express doubts about what Jewish tradition says God "commands" us to do?

8

Skokie and the First Amendment

1978
Skokie, Illinois

BACKGROUND

In 1978, a band of Nazis led by Frank Collin announced plans to march in uniform through the streets of the largely Jewish Chicago suburb of Skokie, whose residents included many survivors of the Holocaust. In response the Skokie community launched a legal campaign to keep the Nazis out, realizing that the showdown was certain to attract national media coverage. Jews from New York to California vowed to mount a counter-demonstration if the Nazis carried out their threat to march. The American Civil Liberties Union, an organization which receives a great deal of its support from Jews, agreed to defend the Nazis. As a result, many Jews tore up their ACLU cards in protest. This came as a surprise to the ACLU. In the 1960s, Jewish ACLU leaders had not complained when the organization defended George Lincoln Rockwell, the notorious founder of the American Nazi Party, who certainly posed a much greater threat than Collin, who was just one of Rockwell's self-styled protégés.

All of the legal and legislative effort to bar the Nazis from demonstrating in Skokie came to naught. Even the Supreme Court of the United States refused to stay the march. In the end the Nazis themselves decided to cancel their appearance in Skokie, originally planned to celebrate Hitler's birthday. Some twenty-five uniformed Nazis did hold a rally later in a Chicago park before an audience of more than 2,000, many of whom were hostile but more of whom apparently were sympathetic to the Nazis. Numerous arrests followed for disturbing the peace. Frank Collin, the leader of the National Socialist Party of America (whose father is Jewish and a concentration camp survivor), was said to have declared: "I believe there was no Holocaust. But they deserve one and they will get it."

THE THREE POSITIONS
Libertarian
Essentially there are three basic positions with regard to the question of Nazi rights under the First Amendment. Framing the question differently, what limits, if any, ought to be imposed on the right to freedom of expression of any group under the First Amendment? The answer given by the American Civil Liberties Union is quite clear. The right to speech and other peaceful means of expression is absolute, no matter how loathsome such expression may be to others. As the ACLU sees it, these rights would be meaningless if government were allowed to pick and choose the persons and groups to whom they apply. Hence the ACLU defends the right of every group to make speeches in which they express their beliefs, to print and distribute written material, to hold peaceful marches and rallies, to display their symbols, and to be members of groups which promote the doctrines in which they believe. It is not the rights of Democrats and Republicans that need protecting, they stress, but rather the rights of the most detested among us.

In the ACLU's view, it is dangerous to make exceptions to First Amendment freedoms, particularly if restraint is imposed on expression before it ever happens. Many people would just love to suppress the groups that they abhor. As far as the Nazis are concerned, according to the ACLU, they are fringe groups of misfits who should be treated with contemptuous indifference, not suppression, and tolerating them is part of the price to be paid for living in a free society.

Jewish Defense League

At the other end of the spectrum is what might be called the Jewish Defense League position, namely that the Nazis should have no right to spread their position. The message of the swastika to Jews is "We want you dead, and we aim to kill you when we can." As the JDL sees it, to maintain that expression of this hateful nature should be protected by the First Amendment is total madness. To consider the question of whether or not the Jews ought to be exterminated as one about which reasonable persons may differ and deserving to have both sides fairly presented in the marketplace of ideas is intolerable. In this view, America should not and need not put up with Nazis anywhere, because if it does it automatically gives them a certain legitimacy to which they cannot conceivably be entitled. Furthermore, the logic of this kind of libertarian liberalism is that ultimately it would be better to be ruled by Nazis (if enough people were persuaded by them) than to restrict their right to speak in any way. An editorial in the *Washington Star* labeled this type of thinking "kamikaze constitutionalism."

"It Depends"

A third and middle-of-the road position on the Nazis is what has been described as the "it depends" position. This position holds that while the Nazis certainly should not be totally suppressed, neither should they be allowed to demonstrate in a place like Skokie. In this view, it is appropriate for government officials to consider the totality of any proposed march or demonstration—factors such as time, place, content, nature, purpose, police capabilities, as well as the probable consequences of such demonstrations. The final say, of course, on any proposed demonstration that is challenged would be up to the courts. It was this philosophical stand that was taken by the late Justice Hugo Black, one of the staunchest defenders of the First Amendment ever to grace the United States Supreme Court. He remarked in a concurring opinion in *Gregory* v. *Chicago* in 1969: "I believe that the homes of men, sometimes the last citadel of the tired, the weary and the sick, can be protected by government from noisy marching, tramping, threatening picketers, and demonstrators intent on filling the minds of men, women and children with fears of the unknown."

DECISION

There is simply no one perfect answer to the problem of the rights of Nazis under the First Amendment. Each of the three enumerated positions has merit, while each is also vulnerable to attack.

DEBATE

Now that you know the facts about the case, you will have a chance to debate your point of view. Choose persons to serve as members of the ACLU, representatives of the Neo-Nazis, and citizens of Skokie. Allow them to debate their case before a judge, and let the remainder of students serve as the jury in the case. Once the case is decided and students have an opportunity to debrief, you may wish to examine the questions that follow and discuss them with your teacher and classmates.

Questions to Think About

1. The National Socialist Party design for its projected appearance in Skokie consisted of a demonstration of thirty men in full uniform including swastikas in front of the village hall with pronouncements no more inflammatory than "Free speech for white people too." If the Nazis had insisted on their right under the First Amendment to parade through Skokie shouting "Kill a Jew today," do you think it would make any difference to the courts? Is there a place where you would draw the line on freedom of expression and speech?

2. In 1978, in Houston, the American Nazi Party arranged a recorded message for anyone who phoned its regular telephone number. The message consisted of language such as "We are now offering a $5,000 prize for every non-white carcass killed while attacking a white person. We are encouraging mass execution of non-whites in order to make their stay in this country an unhealthy one." The message made it clear that non-whites included Jews. If you were a member of the American Civil Liberties Union, would you defend the Nazis' rights to such speech? (Interestingly, the decision was made by the ACLU not to defend the Nazis on the basis that the offering of a bounty transformed this speech into an overt act and thus was not protected under the First Amendment. Some ACLU leaders held the opinion that even such language by the Nazis warranted their defense.)

3. In 1976, a Nazi group in San Francisco opened a storefront called the Rudolf Hess Book Store with a picture of Adolf Hitler in the window. They chose to locate it across the street from a synagogue which included many Holocaust survivors among its members. Shortly after its opening a group of Jews burst into the store and smashed it to bits. That, of course, was against the law. If instead of taking the law into their own hands, the Jews in question had approached a legal defense agency for help, what should the response have been?

4. In Boston, two decades ago, in a desegregated public school a busload of black children arrived for the first time at a previously all-white elementary school. As the children were getting off the bus, they were greeted by white teenagers and adults who shouted obscenities and numerous racial slurs, such as "Niggers, we don't want you here. Go home and don't come back." In your opinion, should this type of expression, in this context, be viewed as protected speech? Why or why not?

5. Milton Ellerin, a specialist on organized anti-Semitism, said that in hindsight the net effect of the Skokie incident was a plus for the Jews, projecting an image of them as a people who are willing to stand up and fight when threatened. Do you agree with this statement? Is the Skokie incident a plus or minus for the Jews?

6. In the nineteenth century, a major source of anti-Semitism was the negative image of the Jew prevalent in popular culture. Americans were inundated with damaging stereotypes of the immigrants' social and personality traits. For example, popular novels and the theater exploited the theme of the Jews as crude, greedy, petty criminals. Do you think that such negative images of Jews are still prevalent

today? Have you encountered any anti-Semitic incidents? Share them with your teacher and classmates.

7. In your estimation, what are the greatest dangers posed by hate groups? How can they be neutralized?

8. The First Amendment to the Constitution of the United States reads: "Congress shall make no law respecting an establishment of religion, or prohibiting the free exercise thereof; or abridging the freedom of speech, or of the press; or of the right of the people peaceably to assemble, and to petition the government for a redress of grievances."

First Amendment rights were at issue in the neo-Nazi march. The law allows for peaceful assembly and the right to free speech. In carrying out the law, however, do you think the rights of others were violated (Jews and other victims of the Nazi terror)? Should freedom of speech be limited in any way?

9. Draft guidelines for the exercise of First Amendment rights which protect all parties in a case such as that of Skokie.

9

Hillel vs. Shammai
The Great Hanukkah Debate

30 C.E.
Babylon

BACKGROUND

In Jewish life Hillel is remembered as the perennial opponent of Shammai. The Talmud records numerous disputes between the two men, and later their disciples. Although each school had a large number of students and followers, Jewish law almost always rules in accordance with Hillel.

A most unusual tale (Eruvin 13b) explains how this came about:

> A heavenly voice declared: "The words of both schools [Hillel and Shammai] are the words of the living God, but the law follows the rulings of the School of Hillel," because the Hillelites were gentle and modest, and studied both their own opinions and the opinions of the other school, and always mentioned the words of the other school with great modesty and humility before their own.

Most of Hillel and Shammai's disputes were about matters of ritual. This case will present a debate between the two schools regarding the correct way to light the hanukkiah on the festival of Hanukkah.

The Hanukkah menorah, today called a hanukkiah, is the candelabrum designed to hold the lights of Hanukkah. It is an adaptation of the ancient menorah of the Jerusalem Temple, one of the earliest symbols of the Jewish people.

Described in detail in the Bible (Exodus 25:31–37), the menorah was said to be a physical representation of the Tree of Life in the Garden of Eden. It had seven branches, which was often seen as representing the seven days of creation. The central lamp of the menorah was never allowed to burn out. This is the source of the *ner tamid* (eternal light) we find today in modern synagogues.

The Temple menorah burned pure, beaten olive oil, oil that was produced in olive presses supervised by representatives of the priesthood. The oil was packaged in containers and sealed with the special mark of the high priest to distinguish it from ordinary oil. This requirement, of course, is an important part of the famous one jug of oil legend of Hanukkah.

When Judah Maccabee decreed an eight-day holiday to commemorate the rededication of the Jerusalem Temple, Jews began to kindle the eight lights of the festival. At first people would simply line up ordinary clay oil lamps. But since multiple lamps of this type were required, the need for a single lamp with multiple wicks became evident.

The difference between the Temple menorah and the hanukkiah is the number of branches. The Temple menorah had seven branches, while the later hanukkiah has nine branches. The early hanukkiah burned olive oil. It was probably made of either stone or metal. Since the hanukkiah was originally placed outside the entrance of the household, lanterns were probably used to protect the flames from the wind. Similarly, back walls developed in the hanukkiah dating from the thirteenth century in order to facilitate the hanging of the hanukkiah on a wall or doorpost.

While eight lights are required by Jewish law on the hanukkiah, it became customary for the hanukkiah to have places for nine flames. The ninth flame is called the *shamash*, or servant. Its purpose is to light the other lights, since Jewish law asserted that the Hanukkah lights themselves were not to be used for any other purpose than to publicize the miracle.

DECISION
Lighting the hanukkiah is the major ritual act of Hanukkah. What you may not realize is that there was a great debate among the disciples of two of the most famous rabbis of the Talmud concerning this practice. Following is the teaching as it appears in the Talmud (Shabbat 21b):

> Our rabbis taught: The precept of Hanukkah demands one light for a man and his household; the zealous kindle a light for each member of the household; and the extremely zealous—Bet Shammai maintain: On the first day eight lights are lit and thereafter they are gradually reduced. But Bet Hillel says: On the first day one is lit and thereafter they are progressively increased. Rabbi Jose ben Abin and Rabbi Jose ben Zebida differ. One maintains: The reason of Bet Shammai is that it shall correspond to the days still to come, (i.e., each evening one must kindle as many lights as the number of days of Hanukkah yet to come), and that of Bet Hillel is that it shall correspond

to the days that are gone. But another maintains: Bet Shammai's reason is that it shall correspond to the bullocks of the festival, while Bet Hillel's reason is that we promote in matters of sanctity but do not reduce.

The reasons the Talmud gives for the disagreement between Shammai and Hillel are instructive. First, it gives the obvious reason. Shammai thought the candles should represent the number of days of Hanukkah still to come, while Hillel thought that it should represent the days already fulfilled. But then, unsatisfied, the Talmud suggests that Shammai had in mind the fact that on Sukkot, while the Temple stood, there was a sacrifice of bulls in which the number of animals killed was reduced by one on each of the seven days of the festival. Perhaps Shammai had in mind that Hanukkah was originally a substitute Sukkot. In any case, the Talmud explains that Hillel argued that we should increase holiness rather than diminish it. A modern sensibility, taking into account the sense of Hanukkah as the turning point from darkness to light, might speculate that in these normal times the normal human fear of darkness would be best assuaged by increasing light. But that after the Messiah comes, when our practice will follow Shammai, human beings will be able to honor and celebrate the divine mystery that resides in darkness.

To reiterate, why are there two candlelighting traditions in the Talmud? There are two answers: the practical and the ideological. The practical reason for the two suggestions is that the rabbis probably did not really know how to do the ritual. It had developed among the people, and different groups most likely followed different practices. The ideological reason reflects one of the great hallmarks of Judaism—its embrace of pluralism. Although the rabbis had to settle on one practice, they included the discussion and reasoning of both traditions in the official record of their deliberations.

DEBATE
It is now your turn to debate the issue of how to properly light a hanukkiah. The debate will take place in early rabbinic times during the time of the lives of the schools of Hillel and Shammai. Choose several persons from the school of Hillel who will seek to argue the point that the correct way to light the hanukkiah is to add an additional light each night, beginning with one light the first time. Choose several persons to be in the school of Shammai and have them argue Shammai's view that the hanukkiah should have all eight candles lighted the first night, seven the second night, and one fewer candle each successive night.

In addition, you may also choose to debate other aspects and laws about the hanukkiah, including its shape, where it ought to be placed, how long the candles ought to burn, and so forth.

Fast Facts
1. The hanukkiah may be made out of any material. Metal, ceramics, and even wood are common.

2. An early midrash records that when the Maccabees entered the Temple they found eight spears left by the Greeks from which they fashioned the very first hanukkiah—a kind of prototypical beating of spears into eternal light.

3. It is preferred, according to Jewish law, that the receptacle of the lights of the hanukkiah form a straight row, not a circle or semi-circle, lest the flames appear as a torch.

4. It is a mitzvah to publicize the miracle of Hanukkah. Placing the hanukkiah on a window sill or even outdoors allows others looking in to see it. The Talmud (Shabbat 21b) is even more specific as to where the hanukkiah ought to be located:

> One should place the hanukkah lamp by the door of the house, on the outside, within a handbreadth of the door, so that it is on the left side of a person entering the house, the mezuzah on the right and the hanukkah lamp on the left. If one resides in an upper story, the lamp should be placed in a window overlooking the public domain. . . . In times of danger, one may place the hanukkah lamp inside the house, on the table.

5. According to talmudic law, each household is to light (at the very least) a single candle on each of the eight nights. In the homes of the very zealous, each member of the family lights one candle every night. The most zealous light one candle on the first night and one additional candle each subsequent night.

6. According to many rabbinic authorities the Hanukkah candles must burn for a minimum of a half-hour.

Questions to Think About

1. It has become a North American tradition to maximize the Hanukkah experience by giving gifts for eight days, decorating one's house with Hanukkah decorations, and the like. How do you feel about this custom? What are some ways of finding additional meaning in each of the eight days of Hanukkah?

2. How do you feel about a public lighting of a large hanukkiah in the town square of a community? Does a hanukkiah belong there?

3. Do you think that Hanukkah ought to be taught or celebrated in some way in the public schools?

4. Pretend that you lived back in the time of Hillel and Shammai and were asked to be part of design committee for a candelabrum to be used for the festival of Hanukkah. What would your hanukkiah look like? Detail the reasons for your design.

5. Which method of lighting the hanukkiah do you prefer—that of Hillel or Shammai? Why?

10

Hasidim vs. Hellenists

165 B.C.E.
Israel

BACKGROUND

In the year 336 B.C.E., Alexander the Great, the king of Macedonia, assembled a large army and crossed from his native Greece into Asia. He crushed the troops of Darius, king of Persia, and thus became ruler of the entire Persian Empire, which included Syria, Palestine, and Egypt.

In 323 B.C.E., Alexander the Great died. His great empire was divided into three kingdoms. There was war between two of these kingdoms, Syria and Egypt, for almost a hundred years. Israel was forced to serve as a land bridge between these two kingdoms and it was torn by the invading armies.

Finally, the war ended, leaving Syria in possession of Israel. Once more peace came to the Jewish state, but it was a peace that was dependent on the whims of the Syrian kings. And it was the whim of such a king that destroyed the peace once and for all, providing us with what was to become known as the festival of Hanukkah.

The Seleucid kings of Syria sought to win Palestine from the Ptolemies of Egypt. The Ptolemies ruled Egypt and Judea. After numerous battles the Syrian king Antiochus II defeated Ptolemy V of Egypt in 198 B.C.E. Antiochus III reduced taxes and guaranteed that Jewish law would be respected. Conditions worsened when his son Antiochus IV ascended the throne in 175 B.C.E. He doubled the tax burden on Judea and abused the Jewish religion.

The Seleucids (ruling Asia Minor and Syria) were Greeks, and like the Ptolemies of Egypt they promoted and spread Greek culture. Antiochus IV took steps to induce the Jews to adopt Greek customs. All of the important government posts went to those who complied. It was not too long before Greek ideas and the Greek way of life had become very fashionable among many of Judea's wealthy nobles and merchants.

Gradually the people of Judea divided into two factions. Those who adopted the Greek way of life and Greek religious practices were called Hellenists. Those who continued to adhere to the laws of the Torah were called Hasidim ("Pietists").

The Hellenists were willing to abandon Judaism in order to be accepted by their pagan rulers. They began to enjoy the philosophy, poetry, art, and music of Greek culture. They gave up their Jewish names and adopted Greek ones, and they stopped circumcising their sons.

On the other hand, the Hasidim believed that Greek paganism and social practices would lead to immorality. They asserted that Greek idol worship, love of conflict, and tolerance of drunkenness would weaken the Jewish way of life. At times there were violent confrontations between Hasidim and Hellenists, who often urged their fellow Jews to use the Greek language and worship Greek gods.

The situation came to a head during the reign of Antiochus IV. He hoped to build his kingdom into a great power, but his dreams were threatened by the Roman Empire rising in the West. The Romans had conquered Greece and Macedonia and marched on to Asia Minor. The Seleucid army was unable to stop them. As a result, Antiochus lost some of his western territories to Rome.

In order to raise funds to defend his kingdom against the growing Roman threat, Antiochus imposed high taxes on Judea to help defray the expense of hiring mercenary soldiers. In addition, he humiliated the Jews by placing a statue of himself in the Temple and forcing the Jews to bow down to it.

Eventually, Antiochus outlawed Judaism. It became a serious offense to observe Jewish laws. The Torah was a forbidden book. The Sabbath, festivals, and holy days could no longer be celebrated in public. Antiochus added the Greek word *Epiphanes* ("God made manifest") to his name. Many Judeans, however, referred to him as Antiochus *Epimanes*, "Antiochus Madman."

The first stirrings of revolt came in the village of Modi'in, where there lived a priest named Mattathias from the Hasmonean family. Surrounded by his five sons, Mattathias walked up to the heathen altar. A Jew who collaborated with the Syrians had just bowed to the idols. Mattathias raised his sword high and his voice came out loud and clear: "He who is with God, let him come with me," he shouted and slew the traitorous idol worshipper. The long-awaited revolt had begun. Mattathias, his sons, and their followers fled to the mountains and joined forces with the Hasidim.

Mattathias died soon after the beginning of the revolt, but his five sons—Judah, Yochanan, Simon, Eliezer, and Jonathan—took over. The commander was Judah, who was called Hamakkabi—"the Hammerer." The people of Judea rallied to the cause of the sons of Mattathias, now known as the Maccabees.

Judah Maccabee conducted a classic guerrilla warfare campaign, striking here and there, attacking whenever feasible. He defeated a Syrian unit based in Samaria and later ambushed a sizable Syrian column passing through the narrow pass of Bet Horon. The Syrians, taken by surprise, were routed. They fled in wild disorder, leaving their weapons and equipment behind. At the Syrian encampment at Emmaus, Judah and 3,000 men made a surprise attack. Unable to rally in time, the Syrians again took flight. Losses were heavy and the Jews had won another great victory against the greatest of odds.

The victorious Jews set about cleaning their house of worship. Judah Maccabee and his men were assisted in this task by the priests and the people of Jerusalem.

On the 25th day of Kislev in 165 B.C.E., three years after its desecration, the Temple in Jerusalem was rededicated. The golden menorah was lit once more.

Tradition tells us that the victors found only enough oil in the Temple to keep the menorah burning for one day. Yet miraculously it burned for eight days. The eight-branched menorah of today and the annual eight-day celebration of Hanukkah, the Festival of Lights, commemorate the victory won for freedom by Judah Maccabee and his courageous followers.

DEBATE
It will now be your opportunity to argue the case for one of two parties, the party of the Hellenizers and the party of the Hasidim, at a conference. Students are to be selected for each group, and each of the parties will then have an opportunity

to present its position. Each position should be argued logically and convincingly. Students will decide who among them will present the position paper. They will also be asked to prepare a party banner and appropriate slogans expressing the party positions. They may also choose to write a song that expresses the party's position.

Both groups come to the conference. Party representatives (those who will deliver the position papers) should sit at a dais in the front of the room. Each party sits together in a separate section of the room. A moderator explains the conference rules. The importance of listening carefully to each group's presentation in order to vote on a policy for Judea must be emphasized here. The conference will proceed as follows:

1. The moderator explains conference procedure and may wish to appoint a secretary to record the major points of each presentation on poster boards.
2. Each party will be called individually.
3. When called upon, the designated representative must make the presentation within no more than four minutes.
4. Each party then has three minutes to stage its demonstration (e.g., sing its song, display its banner or signs).

Fast Facts
Hellenizers

The time has come to get rid of the old-fashioned and outdated Jewish customs and rituals. The Greeks have a much better and more modern way of life. They have sophisticated philosophers and outstanding artists and musicians. The time has come to study their ways in great detail in order to learn and live the beauty of Greek culture.

To begin with, we've got to stop naming our children after people in the Bible. There are so many beautiful Greek names. We must learn them and give them to ourselves and our children. Since Greek culture respects the body, we've got to spend much more time on our appearance. The Greeks wear clothes that fit the times, and their men work to improve their bodies through sports. When our bodies get in shape, it will be time to appear, like them, naked in public places.

We must immediately stop the barbaric ritual of circumcising our sons. If we continue doing this, we'll never be accepted by the Greeks. Temple services are boring. The Greek way is exhilarating. It's time to change the rules of the Sabbath too, and there surely is no reason to keep kosher any more. We will also have to decide what to do with those old-fashioned Hasidim, who are so rigid and fanatical that they think that nothing can or should ever change.

As for our holidays, the Greek ones are far superior. We must learn their customs and rituals, for their way is the way of the future. It's time to be Greek, and convince the rest of the world that the Greek way is the best way!

Hasidim

We are members of an ancient people, the Jewish people, founded by Abraham our father and Sarah our mother. The Greek Hellenizers are trying to convince some of our people to stop our traditional way of life and give up our covenant with God. But we just will not do it. We can't ignore the Hellenizers, for they are still our fellow Jews whose thoughts have simply gone astray. If we fight them, we will be fighting against our own brothers and sisters. But if we don't fight them and what they stand for, soon there will be no Jewish people. It's hard to know exactly what to do.

But we can now see the writing on the wall. Antiochus has taken our Temple away, replacing it with false pagan gods and puppet priests. Soon Jerusalem, the holy city, will become a Greek one and we will be totally banned from it. We must have faith that God will not forsake us. We must speak out against Antiochus' decrees and his plans. We must prove to the Hellenizers that our way, the traditional way, is the only way to truly survive. Judaism must never change. We will never accept Antiochus' ban on Sabbath observance and Torah study. If we have to, we will do it in secret, but we will not stop our Jewish way.

Questions to Think About

1. Can you think of any modern day "Hellenizers" analogous to those in the Hanukkah story?

2. Who are the modern Hasidim?

3. What are some things about Judaism that you would like to see changed to make it more compatible with your way of thinking?

4. What are today's modern-day Jewish factions?

5. Who are the modern-day Maccabees?

6. As more and more people were put to death, a small group of Hasidim concluded that the only resistance possible was to remain faithful and die for God's commandments. Thus the concept of martyrdom developed into an ideal. Are there any things for which you would die?

7. What, in your opinion, is the lesson of Hanukkah?

11

The Trial of Adam and Eve

Beginning of recorded time
Garden of Eden

BACKGROUND

God creates Adam and Eve on the sixth day of creation and places them in the Garden of Eden. In the middle of the garden, God places the Tree of Life and also the Tree of Knowledge of Good and Evil. God tells man and woman that they may eat of every tree in the garden, but must not eat of the Tree of Knowledge of Good and Evil, for if they do, they will die.

In chapter 3 of the Book of Genesis, the shrewd serpent challenges God's command to Adam and Eve, telling them that if they eat of the tree they will not die. The serpent goes on to tell them that as soon as they eat of it their eyes will be opened. "When the woman [Eve] saw that the tree was good for eating and a delight to the eyes, and that the tree was desirable as a source of wisdom, she took its fruit and ate. She also gave some to her husband [Adam], and he too ate of it" (Genesis 3:6).

As a result of their disobeying God's command, Adam and Eve are banished from the Garden of Eden. The serpent is condemned to crawl on its belly for the rest of its life.

In order that everyone may understand the situation which has led to the trial, one person should read aloud

Genesis 2:15–17 and 3:1–13. Following are verses from these chapters:

15. God took man and put him in the garden of Eden to till and tend it. 16. God commanded man saying: "You may eat of every tree of the garden, 17. But you must not eat of the Tree of Knowledge of Good and Bad, for as soon as you do, you will die."

Chapter 3:1. The serpent was the most cunning of all of the wild beasts that God had made. He said to the woman: "Did God really say: `You shall not eat of any tree of the garden'?" 2. The woman answered the serpent, "We may eat of the fruit of the other trees of the garden. 3. It is only the fruit of the tree in the middle of the garden that God said: `Do not eat or touch it, else you will die.'" 4. The serpent said to the woman, "You are not going to die, 5. but God knows that as soon as you eat of it your eyes will be opened, and you will be like divine beings who know good and bad." 6. When the woman saw that the tree was good for eating, and a delight to the eyes, and that the tree was desirable as a fountain of wisdom, she took its fruit and ate. She gave some to her husband, and he ate as well. 7. Then the eyes of both of them were opened, and they realized that they were naked, and so they sewed together fig leaves and made themselves loin-cloths. 8. They heard the sound of God moving in the garden in the breeziness of the day, and the man and his wife hid from God among the trees of the garden. 9. God called out to the man and said to him, "Where are you?" 10. He answered, "I heard the sound of You in the garden, and I was afraid because I was naked, so I hid." 11. Then God asked, "Who told you that you were naked? Did you eat of the tree from which I had forbade you?" 12. The man answered, "The woman you put at my side, she gave me of the tree, and I ate." 13. And God said to the woman, "What is this that you have done?" The woman answered, "The serpent tricked me, and I ate." 14. Then God said to the serpent, "Because you did this, you shall be more cursed than all the cattle and the wild beasts. You shall crawl on your belly, and you shall eat dirt all the days of your life . . . 15. I will put animosity between you and the woman, and between your progeny and hers. They shall strike at your head and you shall strike at their heel." 16. And to the woman God said, "I will make very severe your pain in childbirth. In anguish you shall bear children, and yet your urge shall be for your husband, and he shall rule over you." 17. To Adam God said, "Because you did as your wife told you, and you ate of the tree which I told you not to eat, the ground will be cursed because of you. By toil you shall eat all the days of your life. 18. Thorns and thistles shall it sprout for you. Your food will be the grasses of the field."

DEBATE

A trial has been ordered by the divine council to determine the exact nature of the crime that has been committed and the penalty for that crime in the event that the parties are found guilty. The case will be presented before a jury who will determine the guilt or innocence of the parties. As in any trial, a prosecutor and a defense attorney will need to be appointed. The prosecution will attempt to establish the guilt of Adam, Eve, and the serpent. It will work to prepare a case that will lead to their convictions. It will contend that they have committed a crime against God and therefore ought to be expelled from the Garden of Eden. It may also want to have members of its group function as witnesses for the prosecution. Using imagination, someone from its group may want to play the tree or an animal in the garden or a member of the divine council. The prosecution will ultimately want to show that Adam, Eve, and the serpent had the power to make ethical decisions and therefore did not act out of ignorance. Furthermore, they had been specifically warned not to eat the fruit of the tree. The prosecution will want to try to determine what motives Adam and Eve had for eating the forbidden fruit in order to determine their crime.

The defense will attempt to prepare a case that will lead to the acquittal of Adam, Eve, and the serpent. It will likely want to appoint several defense attorneys as part of its team. It may choose to have someone from its group play a character witness or an expert in moral law. It will ultimately want to show that knowledge of good and evil is essential for life and a necessary part of God's created order. It may also wish to make its case on an order of blame. In that instance, it might fight for the acquittal of Adam and Eve and the conviction of the serpent. Or another possibility is to hold God accountable on the basis that God created everything in the world and must be held responsible and accountable for it.

Following are three interpretations that have been offered by commentators to explain the purpose of the Tree of Knowledge. These interpretations ought to be read by both the prosecuting and defense attorneys to assist them in preparing their cases.

Ethical

Eating from the Tree of Knowledge of Good and Evil provided humans with moral discrimination, thereby making them capable of committing sin. Yielding to the serpent's lure and eating the fruit were two parts of the same act. Once it was done, the relationship between man and God was changed forever. Man's expulsion from the Garden of Eden meant that he could never go back to his previous state of ethical indifference.

Intellectual

In the Bible the expression *tov ve'ra*, "good and bad," is often interpreted to mean "everything." Thus the tale of Adam and Eve may be understood to say that the Tree of Knowledge was the Tree of Omniscience (i.e., knowing all). Having eaten it, man forever after will attempt to know everything. Since Jewish theology posits that only God can know everything, man (in this interpretation) is trying to play the part of God.

Sexual

There are commentators who have read into the Garden of Eden story the discovery of man's sexuality. This is especially suggested by the Hebrew word for "knowledge," *da'at*, which often has the meaning of sexual experience. The story of the expulsion from the Garden of Eden begins with Adam and Eve's discovery of their nakedness and sexual shame. There is thus a link between the Tree of Sexual Knowledge and the Tree of Life. Eating of the Tree of Life would have bestowed man with immortality. That tree is no longer accessible to man, and man must now sustain his species through procreation in the same way as the other creatures of the garden do.

Questions to Think About

1. What do you think God's real intentions were for Adam and Eve? Did God want man and woman to stay forever in the Garden of Eden?

2. If God really did not want Adam and Eve to eat of the forbidden fruit, why did God seem to make the tree so accessible? Why put it in the center of the garden?

3. God said to man and woman that if they ate of the fruit they would die. God did not "make good" on his warning. Why do you think this was so?

4. What do you think God meant when he called to Adam (Genesis 3:9) "where are you?"? Did God not know where Adam was? How do you explain this verse?

5. In Jewish tradition the Garden of Eden has become a projection of the future. In the messianic era people are supposed to return to the harmony of Eden. The Garden of Eden in rabbinic tradition stands for the after-death abode of the righteous. Why do you think that this is so?

6. The Tree of Life, as compared to the Tree of Knowledge of Good and Evil, plays a minor role in this story? Why do you think that this is so?

7. In the story Adam is told that if they eat from the Tree of Knowledge they will die. Eve reports, however, that if they either eat from the "tree in the middle of the garden" or touch it, they will die (see Genesis 3:1–3). Eve not only fails to report the name of the tree but adds this new condition to God's original statement, namely that touching the tree will lead to death. Why do you think that Eve did this? Do you think that her alteration of God's commandment may have led to misunderstanding and ultimately to their expulsion from the Garden of Eden?

8. Adam and Eve each offer an excuse for eating the forbidden fruit. Adam blames God for putting Eve at his side. Eve blames the serpent for tricking her. No one says: "It's my fault." Do you think that the actions of Adam and Eve are in some ways similar to the actions of people today? Who are the modern-day Adams and Eves?

12

The Bar Mitzvah Age Debate

The present

BACKGROUND

Historically the bar mitzvah and later the bat mitzvah represent a Jewish rite of passage when a child reachs the age when he or she is responsible for the performance of mitzvot. According to Jewish law, these new responsibilities occur when a boy reaches age thirteen and a girl twelve.

The actual origin of the bar mitzvah ceremony is shrouded in mystery and scholarly debate. The Bible neither mentions a bar mitzvah celebration nor gives any indication that thirteen was considered the demarcation line between the status of being a minor and an adult. In fact, when a particular age is mentioned in the Bible as a requirement or test for full participation in the community's activities, the age given is twenty, not thirteen.

In the Book of Exodus (30:14) we are told of a census that was taken among the Israelites. Only those twenty or older were to be counted in the census. In the Book of Leviticus (27:1–5) the valuation of individuals for the redemption of vows to God was determined by age. Individuals between the ages of five and twenty were grouped together in valuation, giving some indication that maturity comes at the age of twenty.

The Talmud is also silent with regard to a bar mitzvah at the age of thirteen, indicating that the ceremony as we have it today was unknown in talmudic times. The Talmud, however, does mention the term *bar mitzvah* twice. Both times the reference is to any Jew who observes the commandments and not necessarily to a boy at age thirteen. When referring to a boy of thirteen the Talmud uses the term *bar onshin* ("one who is punishable"). This indicates that a child in talmudic times became liable for wrongdoing at age thirteen.

The clearest and most explicit recognition of thirteen as the age when a child was considered to be a fully responsible member of the community is the mishnaic statement that "at age thirteen one becomes subject to commandments" (Avot 5:21).

There is a vast array of opinions on the reason for the choice of thirteen as the age for performing mitzvot. Some ascribe it to foreign influences present in ancient Israel in the first century B.C.E. Others feel that it may be a throwback to puberty rites that were practiced by many groups. Almost every culture in the world has some kind of initiation rite that heralds a child's entrance into puberty.

DEBATE

In recent years there have been those (especially within the Reform branch of Judaism) who have argued that the ceremony of bar/bat mitzvah ought to be postponed to a later age, possibly fifteen or sixteen, when a person can more fully comprehend the meaning of joining the community and being fully responsible for performing mitzvot. Synagogues that decide to endorse the later age might well require students to study into their teenage years, thus advancing their Jewish knowledge. (It is a fact today that many students

drop out of religious school after becoming bar/bat mitzvah
and do not continue their Jewish education.)

You will now have an opportunity to debate with your
classmates the issue of whether or not to change the age of
bar/bat mitzvah to fifteen or sixteen or to keep it as is.
Students are to be chosen by their teacher to take a side. They
are given time to prepare their statements, and every student
will be afforded a chance to present their case. In addition to
the teacher acting as judge, the teacher may also wish to
select students in the class to act as scorekeepers in the
debate.

At Temple Sholom Hebrew High School in Bridgewater,
New Jersey, we have successfully examined this issue in
debate numerous times. We have found that what works best
is having two teams of three or four students, each of whom
speaks for no more than two minutes. At the end of all of the
presentations, students have time for a rebuttal in which they
may ask questions of the other team and challenge points
that were previously made by the team during the debate.
The judges may score each debater by giving points based on
convincingness, creativity, and number of original points
illustrated.

At the end of the scoring there should be opportunity to
debrief and discuss the issue again, reacting to the suggestions of the debaters.

Questions to Think About

1. Author Herbert Tarr in his book *Heaven Help Us*
describes a bar mitzvah boy who receives a note from his
rabbi which says: "You're going to have to return all of your
gifts, man, if you don't return to religious school. Because I'll
revoke your Bar Mitzvah and declare you a boy again." What

is your opinion of the rabbi's statement? Is it ever possible to revoke one's bar mitzvah?

2. Rabbi Eleazar, the son of Rabbi Simeon, said: "A man is responsible for his son until the age of thirteen. Thereafter he must say: `Blessed is He who has now freed me from the responsibility of this boy'" (Genesis Rabbah 63:10). This statement is still often said today by fathers of b'nai mitzvah in traditional settings. What is meant by this statement? Do you think it still ought to be said?

3. What difference do you think becoming bar/bat mitzvah ought to make in one's life?

4. Following are statements in American law related to responsibility, contracts, serving as witnesses, and guilt of negligence. Remembering that in Jewish law a minor is under the age of thirteen, read the statements and try to understand what being responsible means in American civil law. How does it compare to Jewish adulthood and becoming a bar/bat mitzvah?

(a) In all but two or three states, contracts entered into by a minor (someone under age eighteen) are not binding. This means that if you are under eighteen you cannot buy something on credit, rent an apartment, or buy a magazine subscription.

(b) Someone between the ages of seven and sixteen who commits a crime (i.e., does something which would be considered a crime if an adult did it) is tried in special juvenile court proceedings. (Essentially this means that by definition a child under seven cannot commit a crime.)

(c) The United States Supreme Court decided that it does not constitute cruel and unusual punishment to execute a sixteen-year-old. (Before this decision someone under eighteen could not be executed.)

(d) A child can be a witness in court if the child is considered able to understand what an oath is and what truth and falsehood are. The jury is supposed to take the child's age into account in assessing the reliability of the testimony. (There is a general assumption that a child over twelve is old enough to testify.)

(e) The definition of negligence is failure to meet the standard of conduct which is a reasonable expectation for persons of the same age and intelligence in similar circumstances. If a minor is guilty of negligence which results in damages of any kind, the parents are held liable for compensation.

5. Did you feel that you were old enough to understand the concept of Jewish responsibility when you became bar/bat mitzvah?

6. Are there any suggestions that you might have for improving the significance and meaning of the bar/bat mitzvah for Jewish kids who have come of age?

7. Here is brief selection from Pirke Avot 5:23 that deals with the ages of a person relative to things in one's life. This passage was composed many centuries ago. With which ages do you agree or disagree?

At five years of age, the study of Bible.
At ten, the study of Mishnah.
At thirteen, responsibility for mitzvot.
At fifteen, the study of Talmud.
At eighteen, marriage.
At twenty, pursuit of a livelihood.
At thirty, the peak of one's powers.
At forty, the age of understanding.
At fifty, the age of counsel.
At sixty, old age . . .

13

The Golden Calf
(Guilty or Not Guilty?)

3300 B.C.E.
Mount Sinai

BACKGROUND

Sometime after the exodus of the Israelites from Egypt, Moses ascends Mount Sinai and is given the two tablets containing God's commandments. Forty days have passed and the Israelites begin to grow extremely restless. The people of Israel approach Aaron, brother of Moses, and request that he create a golden calf for them to worship. Aaron agrees, telling the people to contribute their golden jewelry. From this gold a calf is created. The Israelites offer sacrifices before the calf and sit down to drink and make merry.

God proceeds to tell Moses what the people have done and threatens to destroy them. Moses intercedes and argues with God to show compassion and mercy. His argument persuades God not to punish the people.

Holding the tablets, Moses comes down from the mountain. When he sees the Israelites dancing before the golden calf, he shatters the tablets on the ground and burns the calf. Grinding the calf to powder, he sprinkles water on it and forces the Israelites to drink it.

Aaron immediately blames the people, explaining that they requested the idol. He also explains to Moses that he told them to give their gold which he threw "into the fire and out came this calf" (Exodus 32:24).

Judging that the people are out of control, Moses calls upon all who are loyal to God to join him. All of the Levites come forward and following his direction kill those who have demonstrated disloyalty to God. In addition, a plague is sent among the people as punishment for the sin of creating the golden calf.

It is not surprising that many questions and problems have been raised in this Bible story. Why did Aaron acquiesce to the Israelites' demands? Was he too guilty of idolatry and leading the people astray? Why would Moses hurl the holy commandments to the ground, and was he guilty of desecrating holy objects?

DEBATE

Students will now have an opportunity to try both Moses and Aaron in a simulated court of law. Aaron will be tried for his inability to quell the Israelites' demands to build a calf and for his apparent lack of leadership. His brother Moses will be tried for the smashing of the holy tablets and their desecration.

For the trial all participants will need to read the biblical story (Exodus 32:1–35) in order to refresh their memories of the facts and details. The teacher will choose a prosecuting attorney who will attempt to prove the guilt of Aaron and Moses. Also, the teacher will need to choose two students to play the roles of Moses and Aaron and defense attorneys who will be their representatives. In addition, the teacher may choose several other students to play the Israelites who participated in the actual construction of the golden calf. Students also need to be chosen to serve on the jury. If there are not enough students in the class to do this, then it is suggested that parents of the students be invited to serve as jurors.

Following is the biblical story of the construction of the golden calf and the breaking of the tablets by Moses. Pay careful attention to all of the details of the story. They will come in handy during the trial.

1. When the people saw that Moses was taking so long in coming down from the mountain, they congregated against Aaron and said to him: "Come, make for us a god who shall go before us, for that Moses, we do not know what has happened to him." Aaron said to them: "Remove the rings that are on the ears of your wives, your sons, your daughters, and bring them to me." 3. All the people removed their gold rings that were in their ears and brought them to Aaron. 4. He took them from them and threw them in a mold and made into it a molten calf. And they exclaimed: "This is your god, O Israel, who brought you out of the land of Egypt." 5. When Aaron saw this, he built an altar before it. And Aaron announced: "Tomorrow shall be a festival of God." 6. Early next day the people offered up burnt offerings and brought sacrifices of well-being. They sat down to eat and drink, and then they rose up to dance. 7. God spoke to Moses: "Hurry down, for your people, whom you brought out of the land of Egypt, have acted basely. 8. They have been hasty to turn aside from the way that I instructed them. They have made themselves a molten calf and

.bowed low to it and sacrificed to it, saying: `This is your god, O Israel, who brought you out of the land of Egypt.'" 9. God further said to Moses: "I see that this is a stiff-necked people. 10. Now, let Me be, that My anger may blaze forth against them that I may destroy them, and make of you a great nation." 11. But Moses implored God, saying: "Let not Your anger blaze forth against Your people, whom You delivered out of Egypt with great power. 12. Let not the Egyptians say: `It was with evil intent that God delivered them, only to kill them off in the mountains.' Turn from Your blazing anger, and renounce the plan to punish Your people. 13. Remember Your servants Abraham, Isaac, and Jacob, how You swore to them and said to them: `I will make your offspring as numerous as the stars of heaven, and I will give to your offspring this whole land of which I spoke, to possess forever.'" 14. And God relinquished the punishment that He had planned to bring upon His people . . . 19. As soon as Moses came near to the camp and saw the calf and the dancing, he became enraged. He hurled the tablets from his hands and shattered them at the foot of the mountain. 20. He took the calf that they had made and burned it. He ground it to powder and strewed it upon the water, and so made the Israelites drink it. 21. Moses said to Aaron: "What did this people do to you that you have brought such great sin upon them?" 22. Aaron said: "Let not my lord be angry. You know that this people is bent on evil. 23. They said to me: `Make us a god to lead us, for that man Moses who brought us from the land of Egypt, we do not know what has happened to him.'

24. So I said to them, `Whoever has gold, take it off.' They gave it to me and I hurled it into the fire and out came this calf." 25. Moses saw that the people were out of control—since Aaron had let them get out of control—so that they were a menace to any who might oppose them. 26. Moses stood up in the gate of the camp and said: "Whoever is for God, come here." And all the Levites rallied to him. 27. He said to them, "Thus says God: Each of you put sword on thigh, go back and forth from gate to gate throughout the camp, and slay brother, neighbor, and kin." 28. The Levites did as Moses had bidden. Some three thousand people fell that day. 29. And Moses said: "Consecrate yourselves to God this day, for each of you has been against son and brother—that God may bestow a blessing upon you today." 30. The next day Moses said to God: "They have been guilty of a great sin in making for themselves a god of gold. 32. Now, if You will forgive their sin, well and good. If not, erase me from the record which You have written." 33. But God said to Moses, "He who has sinned against me, him only will I erase from My record. 34. Go forth and lead the people where I told you. See, My angel shall go before you. But when I make an accounting, I will bring them to account for their sins." 35. Then God sent a plague upon the people, for what they did with the calf that Aaron made.

Fast Facts

Following are various commentators, both ancient and modern, who have examined the problem of the behavior of both Aaron and Moses and try to make sense of it. Those participating in the trial may wish to use this information as they present their case.

Exodus Rabbah 42:3: According to this midrash, the real sin lay not in the construction of the golden calf but rather in what Israel thought and said when Moses failed to return. Israel said that God redeemed only Himself but not us. God is concerned with Himself but not with us.

Schoenberg: While Aaron wishes to express the idea of God by an understandable image, Moses demands unconditional surrender to an almighty invisible deity. Aaron is convinced that the people will not believe in a god they cannot see. Schoenberg sees this story as the clash between the ideal that the crowd needs to worship and the pure idea of deity—the collision between corporeality and spirituality. When Moses rebukes Aaron because he has tainted the purity of the faith, Aaron points out that the tablets Moses is carrying are also corporeal corruptions of total purity. In sudden despair Moses smashes the tablets, whereupon Aaron rebukes him because the tablets would have helped Israel's faith.

Exodus Rabbah 43:1: ". . . he hurled the tablets from his hands and shattered them . . ." (Exodus 32:19). Moses broke the tablets out of his love for Israel, for as long as the Israelites did not know the Torah they would be judged less harshly. God consoled them, saying: The second tablets will contain much more material—halakhah, midrash, and aggadah.

Martin Buber: This modern philosopher comments on the verse "Let us make a god who shall go before us, for that man Moses, we do not know what happened to him" (Exodus 32:1). Buber asserts that the Israelites were in a state of panic and said to one another: Moses has completely vanished. It must be supposed that this God of his has made away with him. What are we going to do now? We must take matters into our own hands. An image has to be made and then the power of God will enter the image and there will be proper guidance.

Judah Halevi: This medieval philosopher asserts that only 3,000 of the 600,000 people actually requested that Aaron build the golden calf. These people were not real idolaters. In the absence of Moses they were simply desperate to have a tangible object of worship like the other nations without repudiating God who had brought them out of Egypt. Having waited so long, the Israelites were overcome by frustration and confusion. As a result, they divided into angry parties. No longer able to control their fears, a vocal minority pressured Aaron into taking their gold and casting it into a golden calf.

Further, Halevi argues, the creation of the golden calf was not such a serious sin. After all, he explains, making images and using them for worship was accepted religious practice during ancient times. God had commanded the people to create the cherubim and place them above the ark. If the people made a mistake, Halevi argues, it was not in refusing to worship God, but in their impatience.

Adin Steinsaltz: This modern Bible scholar labels the episode of the golden calf the worst failure of Aaron's career. Aaron's guiding principle is peace at any price, compromise to avoid confrontation. For that reason he offers no argument when the people tell him to create an idol. He desperately wants to be loved and to be popular.

Nehama Leibowitz: This modern Israeli Bible professor sees in the golden calf story not only Aaron's failure or the sin of the Israelites but a conscious warning that human beings are capable of acting nobly at one moment and ugly at the next. One single religious experience (i.e., the Ten Commandments) was not capable of changing the people from idol worshipers to monotheists. Only a lengthy disciplining in the laws of Torah could accomplish a true change.

Exodus Rabbah 42:10: Rav Huna believes that Moses intervened on Israel's behalf because he was convinced that their worshipping the golden calf was actually God's fault. The people had not chosen to live among idolaters in Egypt. God had placed them in that evil environment where they had learned bad habits. Thus they were incapable of overcoming the conditions in which they had been reared as children and had survived as adults.

Rabbi Meyer Simcha of Dvinsk: This Hasidic teacher asserts that no object is intrinsically holy. A Torah written by a heretic must be burned because in the final analysis it is the person who endows an object with holiness or profanity. Worshipping an idol, in effect, tainted the heart of the Jews. Since it is the Jews who sanctify the Torah, their idolatry stripped the tablets of their sacred quality. By breaking them, Moses was demonstrating our responsibility for the sanctity of Torah.

Rashi: This medieval Bible scholar quotes a discussion in the Talmud (Shabbat 87a) that makes the point that worshipping the golden calf made Israel strangers to the entire Torah. "If the Passover sacrifice, which is but one of the 613 mitzvot, cannot be partaken of by a stranger, since the Torah said that no stranger shall eat of it, how much more is it true that the whole Torah may not be partaken of by the Israelites when the Israelites are strangers to it." Strangers to the Torah do not need, or want, the tablets, so Moses breaks them.

Rashbam: This medieval philosopher suggests that when Moses comes upon the Israelites and the golden calf, his strength vanishes. It is not so much anger as a profoundly bitter sadness that causes Moses to smash the tablets.

Keli Yakar: This commentator asserts that the tablets are witnesses to a divine revelation between God and Israel, thus publicizing the enormity of their sin. Moses does not want his people to suffer, so he breaks the tablets to mute their testimony.

Questions to Think About

1. Why were the Israelites so impatient with Moses? Why do you think they reverted so quickly to producing their own god?

2. What is your reaction to Aaron's decision to immediately begin to work for the people by asking for a collection of jewelry?

3. What are Moses' compelling arguments to convince God not to lay harm on the Israelites? How do they relate to Moses as a leader?

4. Why do you think Moses cast the tablets to the ground? Was this being a good role model for the people?

5. How would you evaluate the leadership of Aaron in this Bible story? Did he demonstrate weak or clever leadership?

6. Does society today worship idols? What are our modern-day golden calfs?

7. Which commentator's opinion concerning the reason for the Israelites' building a golden calf is most like your own?

8. The mystical book called the *Zohar* suggests that idolatry occurring so soon after the exodus from Egypt reveals to Moses a flaw in his leadership. If the people could sink this low, part of the blame must fall on his own shoulders, and certainly every leader is responsible for training and elevating someone to take his place when he is absent. Moses neglected to do this, and his breaking of the tablets is perhaps his way of sharing in the Israelites' sin and punishment. How do you react to this suggestion? Do you think that Moses bears blame for this tragic story?

9. Moses in this story challenges God and ultimately wins God's forgiveness of the Israelites. Have you ever challenged God? Is it okay to challenge God?

10. There is a rabbinic midrash that tries to protect Aaron's decision to build the golden calf. It is based on the assertion that the Israelite people first asked Hur to build the calf, and when he rebukes them the people kill him. Aaron, seeing the body of Hur at his feet, is fearful for his own life and accedes to the people's wishes. What are your thoughts on this midrash? Do you think that Aaron may have feared for his life in this Bible story?

14

The Trial of Joseph and His Brothers

3600 B.C.E.
Canaan

BACKGROUND

Joseph, a seventeen-year-old lad, helps his older brothers tend the flocks of their father Jacob. Seeing that sometimes they are careless about their responsibilities, Joseph criticizes them to Jacob. Jacob favors Joseph and presents him with a gift of a special coat. Seeing that their father loves Joseph more than he loves them, the brothers greatly dislike Joseph.

One night Joseph dreams that he and his brothers are binding sheaves in a field. His sheaf arises and their sheaves all bow down to it. The next day he tells his brothers about the dream. "Do you mean to rule over us?" they ask, despising him now even more because of his dreams.

On another night Joseph dreams that the sun, the moon, and eleven stars are all bowing down to him. He tells his father and his brothers about the dream. His father scolds him, "What do you mean by such a dream? Are we now all to bow down to you?"

Later in the Bible story Jacob sends Joseph out to bring him a status report on how his brothers are caring for the herds. When his brothers see him coming they plot to kill him. Reuben suggests that they throw Joseph into a pit rather than kill him, hoping that afterwards he might rescue Joseph.

The brothers strip Joseph of his coat and throw him into a pit. As they sit down to dine they see a caravan of Ishmaelites heading toward Egypt. Judah suggests that they sell Joseph, seeing that they have nothing to gain by killing him. The brothers agree and sell Joseph into slavery.

Reuben returns to find that Joseph has disappeared. He tears his clothing as a sign of mourning. The brothers dip Joseph's coat in goat's blood and take it to their father Jacob, telling him that Joseph has been killed by some wild beast. Jacob responds in horror by weeping and tearing his own garments.

There are many problems that arise from the story of Joseph and his brothers. What went wrong with Joseph and his brothers? Why did they feel such anger toward him? What did he do to make them want to slay him and sell him into slavery? Were their actions justified? What was Jacob's role in this drama? Was he guilty of the poor fathering of his sons? Who in this story is guilty and who are the innocent ones?

DEBATE

Students will have an opportunity to try Joseph, his father Jacob, and the brothers before a jury and to determine whether their actions were proper or improper. Did Joseph's actions warrant the reaction of his brothers? Was Jacob an accomplice to this possible crime? Or were the brothers guilty of wrongful behavior to their brother Joseph, having no lawful grounds to sell him as a slave to a band of Ishmaelites?

Participants in the trial ought to include Jacob, Joseph, and the brothers, in particular Reuben and Judah, who play a more important role in the story. Other participants might include one of the band of Ishmaelites, and a jury to determine guilt or innocence. A prosecuting attorney and defense attorney for the characters also need to be chosen.

Following are the pertinent verses from the Bible (Genesis 37) to help the participants in the trial prepare their cases.

2. Joseph, being seventeen years old, was feeding the flock with his brothers . . . Joseph brought an evil report of them to their father. 3. Now Israel loved Joseph more than all of his other children, because he was the son of his old age. And he made him a coat of many parts. 4. And when his brothers saw that their father loved him more than all his brothers, they hated him, and could not speak peaceably to him. 5. And Joseph dreamed a dreamed, and he told it to his brothers, and they hated him yet even more. 6. And he said to them: "Hear, I pray you, this dream which I have dreamed. 7. Behold, we were binding sheaves in the field, and my sheaf arose and stood upright. And your sheaves came around about, and bowed down to mine." 8. And his brothers said to him: "Shall you reign over us and have dominion over us?" And they hated him yet even more for his dreams and for his words. 9. And he dreamed another dream, and told it to his brothers and said: "Behold, I have dreamed yet another dream. In it the sun, moon, and eleven stars bowed down to me." 10. And he told it to

his father and to his brothers, and his father rebuked
him and said to him: "What is this dream that you
have dreamed? Shall I and your mother and your
brother indeed come to bow down to the earth to
you?" 11. And his brothers envied him, but his father
kept the saying in his mind. 12. And his brothers went
out to feed their fathers' flock in Shechem. 13. And
Israel said to Joseph: "Do not your brothers feed the
flock in Shechem? Come and I will send them to you."
14. And he said to him, "Go now and see whether it is
well with your brothers and well with the flock, and
bring me back word." So he sent him out of the vale of
Hebron and he came to Shechem. 15. And a certain
man found him, and behold he was wandering in the
field. And the man asked him: "What are you looking
for?" 16. And he said:"I seek my brothers. Where are
they feeding the flock?" 17. And the man said, "They
have departed." And Joseph went after his brothers
and found them in Dothan. 18. And they came from
far away and before he came near to them, they con-
spired against him to kill him. 19. And they said to
one another: "Behold, this dreamer comes. 20. Let us
slay him, and cast him into one of the pits, and we will
say: `An evil beast has eaten him.' And we shall see
what will become of his dreams." 21. And Reuben
heard it and delivered him out of their hand, and said:
"Let us not take his life." 22. And Reuben said to
them, "Shed no blood. Cast him into the pit that is in
the wilderness, but do not lay a hand on him"—that
he might deliver him out of their hand, to restore him
to his father. 23. And it came to pass, when Joseph
came to his brothers, that they stripped him of his

coat. 24. And they took him and threw him into the pit. The pit was empty, and there was no water in it. 25. And they sat down to eat bread, and they lifted up their eyes and looked, and behold a caravan of Ishmaelites came from Gilead, with their camels bearing spicery and balm and laudanum. 26. And Judah said to his brothers: "What profit is it if we slay our brother and conceal his blood? Come, let us sell him to the Ishmaelites, and let not our hand be upon him, for he is our brother, our flesh." And his brothers listened to him. 28. And there passed by Midianites merchants and they drew and lifted up Joseph out of the pit and sold him to the Ishmaelites for twenty shekels of silver. And they brought Joseph to Egypt. 29. And Reuben returned to the pit, and behold, Joseph was not there. And he rent his clothes, 30. And he returned to his brothers, and said, "The child is not here. As for me, where shall I go?" 32. And they sent the coat of many parts, and brought it to their father, and said, "This is what we have found. Know now whether it is your son's coat or not." 33. And he knew it, and said: "It is my son's coat. An evil beast has eaten him." 34. And Jacob rent his garments, and put sackcloth on his loins, and mourned for his son many days.

Fast Facts

We have seen the results of jealousy and hatred among brothers, beginning with the story of Cain and Abel in the Book of Genesis. Here again we have another story of hostility between brothers. Things in this story become more complicated due to the fact that Joseph's dreams clearly show his superiority to his brothers, causing hatred and jealousy. In addition, the favoritism of father Jacob for Joseph over the other brothers is immediately apparent, further exacerbating the issues. Are the brothers guilty of heinous treatment toward their brother Joseph? What is the level of blame and culpability of father Jacob? Did Joseph's behavior warrant the reaction of his brothers?

There is a plethora of commentaries related to these and other issues. Following is a cross-section of them which ought to be used when preparing the various cases for the trial.

Eli Wiesel: In his book *Messengers of God* Wiesel comments on Joseph's character, asserting that Jacob refused him nothing and that Joseph constantly craved attention. Joseph's arrogance and insensitivity to his brothers' feelings caused their hatred and mistreatment of him.

Genesis Rabbah 84:7: This midrash describes Joseph's concerns for his looks. He used special brushes and pencils to color around his eyes. He put high heels on his shoes so that he would appear taller and perhaps older than his age. Furthermore, he made up stories about his brothers and then told them to his father Jacob. He lied about his brothers in order to make himself look good. For instance, on one occasion he told his father that his brothers were eating unkosher meat and that they were insulting one another.

Rashi: He asserts that Joseph took advantage of every opportunity to gossip about his brothers to his father. Though he certainly knew the truth about what they were doing, he intentionally misinterpreted whatever they said or did to his own selfish advantage. He slandered their intentions as well as their accomplishments. For these reasons, Rashi says, they mistrusted and hated him.

Genesis Rabbah 84:8: In this midrash Rabbi Judah asserts that Jacob favored Joseph because they were similar in appearance. Rabbi Nehemiah thought that Jacob loved Joseph because Jacob spent more time teaching Joseph the fundamentals of his tradition than any of his other sons.

Julian Morgenstern: He asserts that Jacob was at fault for demonstrating greater love for Joseph than for his other sons and for spoiling him. Partiality is always a form of injustice, and injustice is always wrong and causes evil.

Gur Aryeh: He asserts that when Joseph related his dreams, the brothers hatred for him was fanned even more. This is the nature of hatred. Once a new motive is found, additional hostility is felt.

Rabbi Kassel Abelson: He asserts that Jacob's excessive love for Joseph caused Joseph's downfall. He gave Joseph special gifts, exempted him from many tasks assigned to his brothers, listened approvingly to Joseph's prattling about the great future in store for himself, and did not reprove him sufficiently for talebearing against his brothers, or for lording it over them.

Abraham Shtal: Pirke Avot states that "whoever indulges in too many words increases sin." Shtal, an Israeli writer, asserts that Joseph's superfluous words caused the brothers' sin and harmed him and his father.

Questions to Think About

1. In rabbinic literature Joseph is referred to as *Hatzaddik,* "the righteous one." Are there any indications of his righteousness in the Bible story under discussion?

2. What do you believe compelled Joseph to tell his brothers his dreams, the content of which surely would anger them? Why did he need to tell his brothers all of his dreams?

3. Judah said to his brothers, "What profit is there in killing our brother and covering his blood?" (Genesis 37:26). According to the Maharsha, a sixteenth-century Polish commentator, whoever praises Judah for having suggested that money be a consideration in determining Joseph's fate thereby blasphemes God. This is because Judah should have invoked fear of God as the deterrent against committing murder, not consideration of profit. What is your opinion of the Maharsha's commentary? What are your feelings toward Judah and his actions in this story? Of what crime is Judah guilty?

4. Many biblical commentators claim that Joseph was "spoiled" by his father Jacob. It was his father who caused Joseph to begin to think that he was superior to his brothers. What level of guilt do you place on father Jacob in our story?

5. Do you see any similarities between actions of the characters in the Bible story and actions in your own family? If so, what are they?

6. What is the moral of this Bible story?

7. Some commentators have said that Joseph's brothers practice the cruelest of all deceptions, namely the convincing of their father that Joseph is dead. What is your opinion of this statement?

8. Why do you think that Joseph's brothers were so disturbed by his dreams?

9. Rank the characters in this story in order of level of guilt: Jacob, Joseph, Reuben, Judah, the rest of the brothers.